Reviews aı
ſ

Pastor Huebner takes his experience from the classroom and weaves it into a relatable, heart-grabbing, and encouraging book that not only makes teenagers think "I'm not the only one," but also leaves us with a peace beyond understanding. His style of writing along with his ability to squeeze Jesus into the broken corners of our hearts makes this book a must read for every teenager fighting everyday battles, as well as for every adult trying to connect with and encourage the next generation. I would highly encourage all teens to read this book—maybe even twice!"

-Kaylee Mattek, class of 2020

In *Who Am I?* Doctor Huebner appears as a sort of Mr. Rogers who has shown up to speak into the anxious lives of young people, "You are someone. You are loved." A good book is golden for the way it leaves room for a reader to pause and reflect. It leaves space for them to wonder, "Could it be so?"

I will put *Who Am I?* unreservedly into the hands of the young people in my life to create the kind of conversation I most want to have. Phil is consistently engaging and laser-focused on an audience he understands well. He brings a delicate diagnosis of what is really wrong. His writing is beautifully laced with Scripture so as to heal, by the Spirit, every bit as deeply as it wounds. You constantly sense the good place this writer is eager to take his reader, to a life-altering encounter with the truth of Jesus and to a deep realization of our identity in him. This book would have us all truly *know* what we know—our new status and our true worth in Christ—and then each take these things up into an actual life. It means to leave no part of the prodigal heart untouched.

-Rev. Dr. Mark Paustian
Professor at Martin Luther College

"Feelings are not facts." How easily teenagers can fall into the trap of making feelings a personal identity. Pastor Huebner, with his years of experience working with teens, takes some of the most common teenage challenges and confronts feelings with facts, the facts of Jesus Christ crucified and what that means for each individual. He skillfully takes the facts of our identity in Christ and applies them to several individual challenges that teens regularly face. Feelings can go up and down and every which way, but Pastor Huebner points us all to the constant, to the facts, that our identity lies in Christ. This book would be very accessible for a teenager, a parent looking for some talking points, or a pastor working with a youth group. But in reality, the timeless truths of Christ's love in the midst of all challenges will span the generations and drive home "Christ for us" to every reader.

-**Rev. Greg Lyon**
Campus Pastor at Wisconsin Luther College

Pastor Huebner identifies the core problem plaguing everyone, regardless of age: our false self-identity without Christ. From his experiences working with teenagers, he zeroes in on the unique feelings experienced by teens brought on by this false identity in today's world: feeling unloved, guilty, weak, worthless, anxious, alone, among others. He answers each of these feelings by pointedly speaking the facts of Scripture—especially God's saving love in Christ—to the hearts of teens in the language of teens. His extensive and interesting use of Scripture will be appreciated by teens, parents, pastors, and teachers—anyone striving to help teens find real comfort and peace in this troubled world.

-**Rev. Joel Otto**
Professor at Wisconsin Lutheran Seminary

Who Am I?

Understanding Your Identity in Christ Through Facts Not Feelings

Phil Huebner

Edited by Amy Goede

Domus Fidei Publishing
Milwaukee, WI

Copy editing: Amy Goede
Cover design: Carolyn Sachs

ISBN: 978-1-716-56349-2
Ebook ISBN: 978-1-716-54416-3
Library of Congress Control Number: 2020919024

Contents

Introduction   vii

Part 1: Understanding Your Identity

Chapter 1: Why This Book?   3
Chapter 2: Who Am I?   13
Chapter 3: Who You Are   27
Chapter 4: Feelings vs. Facts   43

Part 2: Applying Your Identity

Chapter 5:   I Feel Unloved vs. I Am Loved   63
Chapter 6:   I Feel Guilty vs. I Am Innocent   81
Chapter 7:   I Feel Worthless vs. I Am Priceless   101
Chapter 8:   I Feel Weak vs. I Am Strong   125
Chapter 9:   I Feel Alone vs. I Am Connected   153
Chapter 10: I Feel Anxious vs. I Am Reassured   181
Chapter 11: I Feel Afraid vs. I Am at Peace   207

Part 3: Your Identity Now and Forever

Chapter 12: Feelings Based on Facts   237
Chapter 13: A Not So Little Life Secret   245
Chapter 14: Set Your Mind on Things Above   251

Chapter 15: Quick Reference for Helpful Passages   257

Introduction

"For my thoughts are not your thoughts,
neither are your ways my ways,"
declares the LORD. (Isaiah 55:8–9)

Indeed. Who has known the mind of the Lord or ever understood his ways? I surely do not. Thus, I am continually amazed by the grace of God poured out on this world, and in particular, in my life. I don't personally remember a time when I was not a child of God, but I do know that God has worked in unfathomable ways to make me one. From the perfect timing in world history to send his Son, to arranging all things in history that I might be born in a certain time and place and to working through certain people so that the gospel of Jesus Christ would come to me—this all is too much to grasp. Yet I am thankful.

At the same time, how could I have ever imagined the path God would lead me on in my life? From guiding me into pastoral ministry, to allowing me the privilege of starting a mission church and school from scratch, to planting me now in high school ministry, this too has been astounding. And to think that God would also bless me with such a wonderful wife and incredible children and so many friends to support and sustain me! For a sinner so great as I am, this is nothing less than grace upon grace.

So here I am, with all the unique, brilliant, and loving work of God in my life, now writing a book. I'm not sure I would have imagined myself writing a book but most certainly not on the topic of teens. This too is a testimony to grace. At this moment there is an opportunity for me to reflect on all my personal life and ministry experiences, many of them with teens and families, and perhaps to help point teens to Jesus. For that opportunity and privilege with this book, again, I am so thankful.

When God spoke those opening words through the prophet Isaiah, it was shortly before his famous words stating that as the rain and snow fall from heaven, so his own Word comes out from his mouth and always accomplishes what he desires and achieves his purposes. My prayer then is that God would once more work in unimaginable ways to use his words spoken through me to accomplish what he desires and achieve his purposes among teens.

To that end then, there are two last things to offer—some instructions and many thanks.

How to Use This Book
One of my prayers is that this book can be used often by teens. I would suggest that if this is the first time reading this book, read it all the way through from cover to cover. It's meant to be read like a traditional book.

However, once you have read the entire thing and understand the general concepts of the book, there are some sections you might want to return to. It might be wise to turn from time to time to Chapters 3–4 to review your identity in Christ and how that is guaranteed for you by certain facts.

At other times, you might want to turn to a particular chapter if you are struggling with a certain feeling. For example, I would imagine a teen might think, "I feel so worthless and weak right now," and they might want to reread Chapter 7 or Chapter 8. The Table of Contents can help you navigate to certain chapters that might address certain struggles of the moment. I could see the last three chapters being something worth returning to regularly as well.

I also imagine that there are times when a teen might want a list of Bible verses that can help with certain feelings or struggles. For that reason, I included in the last chapter a quick reference guide with lists of Bible passages to look up in certain situations. Perhaps those alone may be pages worth turning back to frequently.

It is also my hope that this book might be useful to various ministries to and among teens. Churches might want to have this book on hand so that pastors, youth leaders, and lay leaders could use it with teens. The book could also be useful in Christian schools and high schools for those who counsel with or teach teens. It could be given to teens as a helpful resource. Or perhaps those adults in ministry could walk through the book step by step *with* teens. Maybe it could even be used for a teen or youth Bible study.

Finally, I would hope that this book could find frequent use in the home. As much as teens struggle to talk with their parents (and vice versa!!), there might be wonderful conversations and bonding moments if parents and teens worked through the content of this book together.

However the book is used, I pray God blesses it richly and achieves the glorious purposes of his grace!

Thank You!
No project like this would ever be possible without many contributors, even if many of them never touched the document. So many thanks are in order for those who have supported and helped along the way.

I'm so thankful for my parents, Jim and Anne Huebner. They raised and trained me in the faith and modeled a Christian home. They guided me through my difficult teen years, despite how outrageously difficult I was as a teen myself. Dad modeled pastoral ministry for me from young on and was one of the big reasons I wanted to become a pastor. Mom instilled in me a heart that pulsates with compassion for other people. My sister Karis and I are children richly blessed! While talking about parents, I must also express thanks for the continual kindness and generosity of my in-laws, Ron and Mary Pate. Their support and Christian kindness have been such a blessing, and it's easy to see where my wife gets her selfless heart from.

I continue to be thankful for the blessings of Wisconsin Lutheran High School. I hardly know where to start. I would not be who I am today without that school, its diverse and Christian environment, and its loving and dedicated teachers and staff. And of course, the school brought me together with one special classmate who now happens to be my wife! It is a privilege and an honor for my wife and for me to be back at this school on staff as we now serve the next generation of teens. God works in mysterious ways, and I'm enjoying every bit of the journey!

Speaking of high school staff, I can't offer enough thanks to Amy Goede. She has served as an excellent, willing, and enthusiastic editor. To sacrifice time off in the summer and school year to help with this project was very gracious, but also beyond appreciated. Her excellence in editing almost matches her excellence in the classroom and as our English department chair. Her humor and heart were always appreciated as she shared her professional input but also her motherly compassion. My appreciation for her help almost matches my appreciation for her and husband Jason's friendship. In particular, I could never thank her enough for the much-needed friend and mentor she has become to my wife.

Also on the high school staff is the very talented Carolyn Sachs. Regrettably when one is so gifted, they get asked to do a million projects, big and small. Carolyn is one such person. I'm thankful for Carolyn's gifts of creativity and design in service to our high school, but also in her excellent design of the front and back covers for this book. Though for her too, I'm even more so thankful for her friendship.

As for reviewers, I'm thankful to the brothers in ministry and in Christ who were willing to review this work—Rev. Greg Lyon of Wisconsin Lutheran College, Rev. Dr. Mark Paustian of Martin Luther College, and Rev. Joel Otto of Wisconsin Lutheran Seminary. All three are professors at important institutions of higher learning and Christian education. All three are men I respect greatly. Their feedback was helpful and gracious.

I must also mention one special young lady, Miss Kaylee Mattek. I knew of Kaylee when she was just a baby, but I had the privilege of getting to know her, teaching her, and working with her at Wisconsin Lutheran High School. That is, until the Lord led her father to be a pastor at a different church away from the area. We stayed in touch over the next bit of time, and when I thought of having an actual teen review what I was writing, she was the first person I thought of. Her comments and feedback were helpful, thoughtful, and sincere. Her encouragement was appreciated even more. God has blessed this young lady with a fierce faith and a compassionate, selfless heart for others. She has been a blessing to me, and God will surely bless many others through her as well!

While I mention specific people, I must offer thanks to all the teens in general that I have worked with at Wisconsin Lutheran High School. There are too many to name specifically, but if any of you whom we have taught, coached, or served read this book, please know how dearly my wife and I love you all!

Finally, my incredible wife Becky. I don't think I have ever met in my life someone who is more selfless, giving, loving, and compassionate than Becky. Anyone blessed to know her recognizes this in an instant—she will put anyone and everyone before herself, even when it is inconvenient or illogical to do so. And to think that she would love me with such a selfless love! Becky has always supported every crazy ministry idea I have ever had or tried, including jumping into this book project. Every endeavor comes with a response of, "That's really cool . . . That sounds great . . . I'm sure it will be really helpful." I am so blessed to have such a beautiful woman inside and out, a model Christian woman to so many young teen ladies.

Together we are also so blessed to have our children Noah and Gwen. We love them immensely, as crazy as they may be at times. Noah is such a clever, intelligent, and funny young man. I fear he is too similar to me in personality, but I'm thankful for his mother's shaping and influence. I pray that his solid, grounded behavior and faith carry him through his teen years which he just started. Gwendolyn is a firecracker of energy—so athletic, so silly and funny, and so compassionate toward other people. I fear she will give us a run for our money in her teen years, but I am confident that she will be a leader as a fun-loving and caring woman of God, just like her mother.

I wish I had time, space, and memory to list all who need to be thanked. But to all who have supported me, my family, and this project—you do in fact have my sincere thanks.

To God alone be all thanks and praise. To him alone be the glory.

Part 1:
Understanding Your Identity

Chapter 1

Why This Book?

That's a fair enough question.

You've been annoying your parents and teachers for years with that question—Why? "Why is the sky blue? . . . Why do I have to clean my room? . . . Why is a baby in mommy's tummy? . . . Why is my curfew earlier than everyone else's?"

I'm going to be honest. We parents sometimes get *super* annoyed by this. "Really? Another 'Why?' Can't I just get a break from being a living Google all day long?!" Eventually we catch our breath though and realize how important it is for you to ask this. "Why?" isn't just a good question—it's a *great* question. You *should* be asking this question.

As you grow, you are constantly learning and pulling in information and connecting data from all over the place. Not only this, but your mind is developing in abstract thought as you start to make sense of the concrete facts of life. So *why* wouldn't a developing and learning person ask the question "Why?"

I'm glad you asked then, and I hope I am going to answer a lot of your "Why?" questions. Let's start with this one: Why do you have this book?

That's also a good question. I know full well that you could be doing any number of things right now. Certainly, something could be added to your Instagram or Snapchat story—those pics aren't adding themselves. There are plenty of Xbox games to play and online people to play with. There are also more shows on Netflix, Hulu, and Amazon Prime than you could binge

3

watch in a lifetime. Most of you would probably rather scroll through an endless collection of YouTube videos with that glassy look in your eye that comes from mindless digital activity.[1] *Anything* besides reading a book! Especially a Jesus book! Who thinks that's cool?

Why do you have this book in your hands then? I'm going to guess that you probably fit into one of the following categories:

The Forced

If you're this person, someone gave you this book and said, "Read!" Maybe it's a pastor or youth group leader or teacher who's looking out for you. They want to help you out, but they aren't completely sure how, and they've had some trouble relating to you. They don't know what to say except, "Here, read this book and we will talk about it later."

More likely, if you are forced into doing this dreadful thing called "reading," and it happens to be reading this book, it's your parents who are the culprits. If you are forced to read this, it's likely because things haven't been very good at home. To say that you aren't seeing eye-to-eye with dad and/or mom would be the understatement of the year. They aren't dumb though. Usually parents know when something is up.

Perhaps, then, one or both of your parents awkwardly approached you at the most inconvenient and out-of-the-blue time and said, "Hey. I got you something." But your momentary hopes for Chick-fil-A or a bigger data plan blew up in smoke as they handed you this book. "Look, I know things haven't been right lately. I want you to read this book. I think it will help. Read it and we'll talk about it." #whelp

---

[1] Before you do the #OKBoomer thing to me, understand that I am perfectly aware that things like Instagram, Snapchat, Netflix, and even #OKBoomer might well be long gone and no longer cool by the time this is published. Such is technology. So feel free to come up with your own examples and #DealWithIt.

If you were forced into reading this book, I'm sorry. But please don't treat this like just another assignment, and please don't worry! God will bless your reading, even if it wasn't your idea!

The Encouraged

If you're this person, you aren't much different than The Forced person, except that the circumstances might be slightly more cordial. If this is you, then you probably have a very well-intentioned, caring, and compassionate pastor, youth group leader, or teacher who wants to help. They really do care about you quite a bit. They probably thought this was something that could help you in difficult times, so they handed you the book and said, "Here's something that I think could really help you grow in faith. Check it out!"

Or it could be your parents. Dad or mom might not be in tune with you and your life, but they are at least "with it" enough to know that you could use some help. Maybe this conversation was more on the endearing side. "Listen, I can tell that things haven't been right lately. You haven't been acting the same. This is not the "you" we've known for so long. I know you don't like talking to me always, and I don't always know what to say. I found this book though and I'd like you to try it out. I think it can really help you out. Please try it and see what answers God can give you."

Or maybe, just maybe, there was even a friend who read this book and liked it.[2] It helped them through some difficult things—some things they know you are going through. Knowing you could use some godly encouragement, your friend recommended this book or let you borrow their copy.

If any of these situations apply to you and someone encouraged you to read this book—awesome! Be wise. Listen to your

---

[2] If even one teen reads this book, liked it, and was blessed through it, I would be enthralled and consider myself blessed beyond belief!

Who Am I? | Chapter 1: Why This Book?

Christian leaders or parents or friends and keep reading! God will bless it!

The Intrigued

I suppose it is possible that you are a teen who actually does like to read. You might also be a teen that enjoys learning more about Jesus and growing in faith. Or it is even within the realm of possibility that you are the narwhal of teens—you actually like *both* reading *and* growing in faith. That would be amazing!

Then again, perhaps you're just intrigued by the topic. You've been doing a lot of thinking and reflecting about yourself lately. You feel like you are trying to "find yourself" and something about this book or the title caught your attention. "Hmm. What's this about? Could this help? Maybe this will be good for me. Why not? I guess it couldn't hurt."

If you are reading this book because you're intrigued by the topic and the content, great! Stick with it. Again I say that God will bless it!

The Desperate

If you don't fit into one of the previous categories in some way, I'm going to guess that this is you. If so, my heart goes out to you. If you are desperate, you and I both know it has nothing to do with your relationship status. This is all about what's in your heart and mind.

Right now you feel so lost. Life has felt like it's been slipping away from you little by little, but now you're in a really bad spot. If the dam was creaking and cracking little by little, you feel like the water is about to burst through, and you're about to drown.

You don't even know where to begin. Nothing seems to go right. No one seems to understand you. No one "gets you." No one seems to be there for you. At the same time, you aren't really sure who you are anymore either.

6

Maybe you've tried coping with this. Anything from ignoring the problem to soaking your pillow with tears to alcohol or pills or any number of things—but nothing has seemed to help. Not *really* help, that is. Sure, some things may have made you feel better at times. But that's just it—at times. Occasionally. For just a bit. But not *really* help.

It's in those lost, hopeless, and helpless moments that you feel so very desperate. Can some*one* or some*thing* please help! Please!

So here you are with this book in your hands. If you are feeling desperate for help, then I'm glad you have this book. This book, God-willing, will be of great help to you. God will bless it.

One More "Why?"

By this point though, you've probably noticed that I'm speaking rather confidently about this book. "God will bless it!" I keep saying. I say this not because I think I'm such a great writer, though. I'm speaking confidently about this book because we have such a great God. God promises that his Word is *always* powerful and effective.[3] What is more, Jesus has worked wonders of God's grace that all belong to you, and he wants you to know that and own that! And so, yes, I say with full confidence that God *will* bless your reading of this book.

Yet I suppose that leaves one more "Why?" question. Why should you read what I am writing? After all, I'm old enough right now to be a father to any of you teens. If this book is around long enough, in a few decades I would be old enough to be your grandfather. And a few decades after that, God-willing, I won't even be alive anymore. So what do I know about your life or about teens? Why should you read what I am writing?

---

[3] See Isaiah 55:10–11 and Hebrews 4:12. In these verses God tells us his Word is powerful and effective and always achieves its purpose because it is sharp, powerful, and effective like a double-edged sword.

I know you don't have this book to read about me. But you asked a good question, so I'll do my best to honor it with a few brief answers with some info about myself.

I Remember

Contrary to many others of older generations, I actually do remember well what it was like to be a teen. It's weird, isn't it? It's like most people grow up and suddenly they get amnesia of their youth. Sure they remember that one big game they won or that time they narrowly avoided getting into huge trouble when they dove into a bush to hide while toilet papering a house. Somehow though it seems like those same adults lose touch with all the other everyday struggles of teen life.

That's *not* the case for me. I remember my middle school and high school days very well. For me, this was one of the most enjoyable times of my life, a time when I felt most "alive," if you will. But before you think, "Oh great, some guy who had an unrealistically great life in high school is going to try and talk to me about my realistically awful life in high school," think again. High school was in no way cupcakes and frosting all four years for me. In fact, much of it was quite difficult.

I struggled with relationships quite a bit and jumped from girlfriend to girlfriend. I lost my friend group from the first two years of high school and felt quite alone for quite a while. One time I was *the* talk of the town for at least a full week. Everyone heard a rumor about me which wasn't true. Everyone asked me about it. Most made fun of me for it. And it wasn't even true!

I had great successes but also major failures in high school. I didn't want to talk to my parents about any of it though. I didn't always have friends to talk about it. Part of me felt like I was a loser for struggling through such "dumb" stuff, and the other part of me felt like I had to figure it out on my own somehow.

I have not forgotten this. I remember it all very well. But Jesus got me through it all, and I was very blessed by every experience—both the good and the bad. Now that I've learned from all these teen experiences, I want to share what God says with you who are going through many of the same things I did.

I Hear You

If you would have asked me back in my seminary training days what kind of people I would like to serve someday as a pastor, teens would have been one of the last things I would have answered. Probably just above rural farming community in the middle of nowhere or back in my home region of the Midwest, teen ministry would have been barely off the bottom of my list.

It's not that I didn't like teens. I did. The first problem though was that I had trouble relating to them. I liked to hang out and have fun with them. In my intern year at the seminary (we call it the vicar year), I did some things with the youth group. It was awesome to be the somewhat-older, cool pastor-in-training who could still relate to teens. But to be honest, although I liked to hang with them, I never got very involved in the actual lives of teens.

Secondly, my ministry aspirations were in the mission fields. I really wanted to be in a state far away from the Midwest where I could either start a mission church or help one that recently opened. I had a great passion for that. Working with teens was simply not a passion at the time.

As it turned out, it was God's will for me to do mission work. After graduation I was sent to start a mission church in the city of Palm Coast, Florida (it's about halfway between St. Augustine and Daytona Beach by the Atlantic Ocean). For nine years we scratched and clawed as we built up that ministry by God's grace. The congregation grew. We started a preschool and a K-8 school. We built multiple buildings. Of course, we also built multiple programs such as youth and teen groups, too. This was a dream come true, and I loved every minute of it. I thought (OK, sometimes even said out loud), "I would never leave this place!" And to be honest, I would have never *ever* thought I would leave church ministry for high school ministry.

But, oh, that God of ours! He always knows so much better!

Sure enough, after nine years I received a divine call[4] to serve as the Campus Pastor at Wisconsin Lutheran High School in Milwaukee, Wisconsin. What? Teen ministry? Back in the Midwest? Never! Not so fast . . .

This high school is actually the one that I went to *and* my wife was my classmate there. It's very near and dear to our hearts. In addition, for everything I loved about our Florida mission church ministry, the circumstances and the timing all added up to the Lord leading me to accept that calling to move back to Wisconsin and serve among teens.

So here I am today at the moment that I'm writing this. I'm the Campus Pastor at my former high school. This means that I do some teaching of religion classes. I help plan mission trips and daily chapel services and some other things here and there like coaching football and track. But most of my time is actually spent with you—teens.

So let me just say right now, wow did I have everything wrong! I *thought* I knew teens because I taught 6th through 8th graders in Florida, and we had a youth and teen group. But I had no idea. I had no clue what I was missing about the life of teens.

My wife also teaches and coaches at the same high school now, and over the last few years we have been immersed in teen life. We have learned so much! We have listened to you and talked to you. We've seen you bouncing with joy. We've seen you crushed with devastation. We've seen your faces beaming with smiles and your faces soaked with tears. We've seen the good choices and

---

4 divine call = job offer from God through the church

the horrible choices. All the while, we've listened and talked to you about what was going on.

This is one of the biggest reasons I'm writing this book. I hear you! I hear your hurt and your pain and your struggles. I hear how lost you are at times. I hear how much you want help and that you're not sure where to look.

So let me say this again: I hear you! What I've heard and learned from teens my entire life, but especially in these last few years, are the things that have led up to the content of this book.

I Care

All that leads to this final point. I care. A *lot*. Living among you teens and watching you and listening to you has been so enjoyable and fulfilling. Yet it has also been *so* heartbreaking.

I'm reminded of one of my favorite Bible stories—the feeding of the 5,000. I don't love this story only because of the impressive miracle Jesus performed in feeding so many with so little food. Instead, there is one particular verse that touches my heart. Mark tells us that Jesus was being swamped by people—like no personal time or personal space at all. Even when he went by boat across the water to get a little relief, the crowds followed him and swarmed him again!

Yet instead of angrily sending these needy people away, the Bible says this, "When Jesus landed and saw a large crowd, he had compassion on them, because they were like sheep without a shepherd. So he began teaching them many things."[5]

I love this verse! In the original Greek language, that word *compassion* means to love someone deeply from the gut. It's kind of like when you go to that dance with Mr./Miss Dreamy and your heart is all fluttering like butterflies and you feel like you're going to hurl. Or even more, it's when you have someone

---

[5] Mark 6:34

special—family, best friend, long term boyfriend/girlfriend—and you would almost do anything for them in love. That kind of deep-seated, from your gut love is this word *compassion*.

Here's Jesus, then, among all these crowds of people, and what did he do? He looked at them and loved them deeply. Why? Because they were so lost. They were like sheep without a shepherd. "So he began to teach them many things."

Dear teen, that's how I feel about you. I may know you, but most likely I don't. Either way, I want you to know that I have great *compassion* for you! I hear you. I see you. I know. Your life is *so* difficult! Sometimes when I see you it looks like you are lost sheep, wandering around without a shepherd. It breaks my heart! So please know that I care, and I want to teach you many things—Jesus things.

I'm not sure why you have this book. But I'm glad that you do. You have a lot to go through. Teen life is in fact *so* tough! Yet God has worked in all things in your life and in mine so that, for one reason or another, you are holding and (hopefully) reading this book. God be praised for that, and God be praised for the opportunity for Jesus to tell you so much about the identity you can find in him! I may love you, but Jesus loves you so much more!

So by all means, please, read on!

What we will do first is figure out what seems to be the big problem for teens today. Then we'll talk about the solution to that problem. That's Part 1 of this book. After that we'll spend the majority of our time together applying what we learned to your life through real life examples and applications. That's Part 2. Then we'll wrap things up in Part 3 where I'll tie a neat little Jesus bow on top of it all. Soon enough, you'll be on your way to a whole new understanding of your life. God-willing and by his grace, that is. Onward we go then! Let's figure out what the big problem is for teens today!

Chapter 2

Who Am I?

Scene 1

Todd Dailey was having just another day. It was extraordinarily ordinary, and that was totally fine for Todd. He needed an ordinary day for once to bring some calm to his life. Truth be told, things had not been good at home.

Todd was married with three kids—17, 13, and 10—but it was his oldest, Meghan, who gave them the most trouble. She wasn't even that "naughty" per se, but it was Meghan's general attitude that was so draining on the family. Meghan was a typical first child—sometimes sweet, sometimes defiant, usually trying to figure stuff out on her own, and always taking the brunt of her parents' discipline.

For a while the family was dealing with Meghan's transition toward independence and adulthood just fine. But it was her sophomore year that brought in *big* changes. Over the year her mood and attitude changed drastically. Normally sweet and sassy Meghan was now deeply depressed Meghan. She yelled at her parents, if she talked to them at all. She shut out her younger brother and sister from her life, if ever she emerged from behind her closed bedroom door.

All of this was trying on Todd and his wife, their marriage, and the whole family in general. So yeah, a normal day was much needed for Todd.

But that was all about to change in a flash.

Todd finished his "normal" day with his normal routine. He nodded at a few neighbors as his car rolled through the neighborhood. He pulled into the driveway and parked on the right so his wife would have room to park when she got home. He got the mail and flipped through it as he strolled to the front door. He walked in and dropped his keys in the tray.

Then he looked up. And that's when he saw her.

"NOOOOOOO!" he screamed with blood-curdling volume.

Todd saw Meghan curled up in a ball on the kitchen floor with a bottle in her hands and a scattering of pills all over the place.

"No! Please, Lord, no!" he muttered as he swooped into the kitchen and swept his dear daughter into his arms.

Meghan was still alive, but she was shaking and sobbing so violently that more pills were jumping out of the bottle by the second.

"How many did you take? How many did you take?" her father asked with hurried worry in his voice.

"I didn't have any," she mustered out in between sobs. "I couldn't . . . but I almost . . . I wanted to, but then I didn't . . . I don't know. I just don't know. Help, Daddy. Please help. I just don't know who I am anymore." Meghan wanted to burst out: *Who am I?*

Scene 2
Deion was staring blankly at his phone. The blue haze softly lit up his face as he lay there in the darkness of his bedroom. A million different things he could do with that technological wonder, but he wasn't sure he wanted to do any of them anymore. How did it get to this point?

Deion thought back for a moment to middle school. Those were good ol' days because he was "the man" on campus. He was the best athlete in his class. His grades were good. He had fun hanging out with his friends—that is, when he wasn't playing basketball. Most of Deion's life was consumed by sports and especially basketball. His AAU team was dominant in the tournaments they played nearly every weekend.

If only . . . if only he could have those moments back. Things were so much different now. When did everything change?

Deion entered high school with high hopes and all the swagger a young hooper could carry. He wasn't really unnerved by the big student body. He knew he was going to be popular. Who wouldn't love a guy with all the good looks, good humor, and on the fast track to a D-1 scholarship?

However, that bubble burst, no, it exploded in Deion's face in just four months. During November tryouts, Deion walked up to the team list with his usual confidence, but he had to blink twice at what he saw. In fact, he had to go to the coach to make sure it was right. It was. Deion didn't even make the JV-2 freshmen basketball team. How could this be? "Man, that coach doesn't know nothin'!" he said to all his friends.

The rest of that year, over the summer, and into sophomore year Deion used every ounce of adrenaline he had to prove the world wrong. "I'm gonna be great," he would say to everyone. But Deion didn't even make it past the second cut that next time. It turned out that everyone else had surpassed him in basketball talent over the last few years. His dream was officially gone.

"Maybe that was the moment," Deion thought, still staring at his iPhone in the darkness.

You see, from that point on Deion had been in a massively destructive tailspin. All the attention he used to give to basketball and workouts he now gave to his social life. He didn't realize it at the time, but it sure felt good to squash the hurt with popularity.

And boy was Deion popular! He may not have made the team, but Deion still could make all the ladies stare and a room bust a gut in laughter.

Deion got invited to every party. It seemed like every hot girl in school was talking to him on Snapchat. He hung out with upperclassmen all the time. Everyone seemed to love him. Even the homecoming queen wanted to go with Deion to the dance when he was only a junior.

What a night that was! The dance was good, but the afterparty was LIT. First a few bottles of alcohol came out. Deion wasn't sure he wanted to drink, but quickly he realized that alcohol heightened his humor and made others laugh even more at him. Then Deion and Miss HOCO Queen herself found their way to some privacy where they made out and messed around a little bit. Then by the end of the party as they were chilling in the backyard, one of Deion's longtime friends suddenly had a bag of pills in his hands. Deion didn't remember too much after that.

Now a senior, Deion was in deep and he knew it. In his honest moments—moments like this where he was alone in his room and left to his own thoughts—it would eat him alive.

So there he was, staring at his phone. He knew he could scroll through his contacts and in seconds one of his plugs would be on the way with any kind of pill, joint, or drink he wanted. Yet he had this feeling deep inside that someday he was going to go way overboard and hurt himself. He probably already crossed the line way too often.

At the same time, Deion knew he could hook up with any number of girls. In fact, his heart started racing a bit as he thought about the two girls he had slept with before. And when the real thing wasn't available, Deion had an Instagram account filled with filth, and a browser history that was even worse.

There, in that quiet moment in his room, it seemed like a mountain of guilt was suffocating him on his pillow. How did it get to this point? Was he even a Christian anymore? Did God still love him? Did he still have faith? He almost wanted to scream: *Who am I?*

Scene 3

Grace was disgusted. Disgusted with herself. Disgusted with her situation. Disgusted with her "friends"—at least the friends she *thought* she had.

Yet another post, yet another failure. Couldn't someone show her at least a *little* love? Someone? Anyone? She tried. She tried *really* hard.

Every time Grace took a selfie she made sure the lighting, the pose, and the look were just right. If they weren't, she took the pic again . . . and again . . . again. When she was finally satisfied with the selfie, Grace painstakingly airbrushed away every blemish on her face and tediously scrolled through all the filters to find the cutest one possible. Then came the dreaded part— the caption. Grace knew her caption game was weak. Yeah, it was only a few words, but how come everyone else had clever or hilarious words pouring off their fingertips when the best she could come up with was "Lazy Dayz" or "Fun with Friends"? She probably typed and deleted and retyped more than 50 caption words every time she tried to post.

After all that time and after all that effort, Grace eventually was satisfied enough to share the post. Within seconds she also added to her story in big, bold words—GO LIKE MY RECENT. She cross-posted the self-promo, too. Maybe this time she would get a few more likes. Maybe this time her picture was so perfect that she looked at least *close* to as beautiful as the known school hottie Amayah. Maybe. Right?

Two disappointing days passed before Grace reluctantly admitted that another post had bombed. Really? Only 26 likes? That's it? In two days?? The backup goalie on the soccer team gets over 100 in like 5 minutes. Only 26? Grace debated what would be more embarrassing—deleting yet another post or leaving it up with so few likes for everyone to see. Yet even if no one else noticed or knew about her Insta-failure, she sure did.

What Grace seemed to know, or at least had convinced herself, was that she simply was not cool at all. She considered her number of followers and likes as Exhibit A of her evidence. But that was just the tip of a nasty social iceberg.

Grace would see endless pictures from pre-dance photoshoots and sleepovers and post-game parties, but she wasn't in *any* of them. She wasn't even invited. "Hey, you should come sometime!" almost made her cringe when other people said it. "Why can't someone just invite me for real to something?" she thought.

Even worse, Grace tried inviting some of her friends to hang out. But for some reason Olivia always had something "just come up" with family or friends and never could do anything. And Emily, Grace's best friend since preschool, always seemed to shoot her down, too. Come to think of it, Emily hadn't done anything with her for over a year. And sure enough, twice in the last month Emily had said she was "too busy" to hang out, only for Grace to see Emily hanging with other friends on her Snapchat story each time!

Her friends didn't like her. Boys didn't notice her. She couldn't even get a stupid click or like on social media.

"What's wrong with me?! Why doesn't anyone like me? Why don't I like me?" Through all the tears, Grace wanted to shout: *Who am I?*

18

An Identity Crisis

I've worked with a countless number of teens now in my years as a pastor, especially in my recent years as the campus pastor at a high school. Due to the nature of my position, I get asked a lot of questions about you. Most of them are pretty obvious and expected:

> What's it like working with teens?

> How do you handle all that drama?

> Ready to go back to a regular church yet?

But of all the questions I get asked, this one is probably the most poignant and important:

> What do you think is the biggest problem for teenagers today?

It only took me a few months into my new gig as a campus pastor to realize that life for you teens is *really* rough these days. Though I didn't know many teens very personally yet, I saw and heard the drama pretty fast. Then as I became more immersed in teen life, the same question was on my own mind—What's going on here? What's the problem for teenagers today?

When people would ask me that question in my first year or two, I had some pretty basic and standard answers.

> "They're totally overwhelmed. They have way too much to balance! The homework load is ridiculous. Especially the advanced, honors, and AP kids. There are so many hours of classwork. Then there are sports and clubs and music programs and their jobs. It's all too much."

OR

"Life is so fast paced now. It's hard for them to keep up with everything, and their parents are far too demanding."

OR

"It's the breakdown of the family units. Far too many homes don't have dad *and* mom present, and those that do have both parents still have poor home environments due to too much stress."

OR

"It's the social media. They're destroying themselves and destroying others every day with that stuff."

OR

"It's all the temptations. There are so many more temptations these days and they can get themselves in a world of trouble faster than ever before."

I'm sure I said all of those things and more when trying to answer that question, and those other adults who didn't really know any better would nod their heads and say, "Oh that totally makes sense. I've always thought that, too!" (no matter which of the above answers I gave them).

But to some extent I regret saying those things. Not that they were bad or wrong. Not that I meant anything bad or mean. It's just that I didn't fully understand you teens yet.

You see, all those things and many more are definitely problems for teens today. I would imagine that any number of you reading this might agree with or experience one or more of the identified problems above. I'm also sure you would have a big list of your own problems to add to the list. Yet while those things are definitely problems for you, I don't believe they are *the* problem.

But I think I know now.

After being submerged in your lives and listening and talking and laughing and crying with you, I think I get it now. I think I finally understand, and I think I know the answer to the question.[6]

What's the biggest problem for teenagers today?

In my opinion, I believe that the biggest problem facing you teens today is this: A *major* identity crisis.

Allow me to explain.

All of those previous problems I mentioned are just symptoms of a bigger sickness. For example, one symptom is getting caught up in popularity—how much or how many people like you in person or online. How people view you, or like your posts, or connect with you (or don't) all really affect how you view yourself.

Another symptom is trying to live up to some kind of imagined expectation of who you are supposed to be. Maybe it's your own dream of being an athlete or the next big singer to catch a break or the pre-med student with all the scholarships. Maybe it's your parents' expectations for what *they* want you to be—some more successful version of themselves that they could never achieve. Maybe you can achieve what they couldn't!

Another symptom is guilt. Lots of guilt. Guilt over what you've done or seen or said or smoked or drank. You have so much guilt that you're embarrassed and ashamed. You're maybe even

---

[6] Well at least I *think* I do. Maybe in a couple years I'll have a new lightbulb pop on and then I'll have to hit you up for another book purchase. Then again, by that time you likely won't be a teen anymore and you'll have life all figured out, right?

beyond the point of caring or trying to stop. You've lost yourself in sin.

Another symptom is sadness, anxiety, or even depression. Your heart feels so troubled or your brain is so overwhelmed that you can't even think straight. For a while you tried to fight it, but now it's too much to handle. This just seems to be the way your life is. You're that sad kid who can't get your life straight.

And so on.

But all these problems are really symptoms of the bigger disease, of the cancer that's growing inside of you. That problem is this: understanding who you really are. Or in other words, **the problem is understanding your identity.**

Do you see this happening in your life? It's easy to tell. When you start to get off track a little (or even *way* off track), it's usually when you start a sentence this way, "I feel . . ."

Now don't get me wrong, feelings aren't bad. And it's good, no, it's *great* to express your feelings. You should be doing that and it's healthy to do that. The problem though is when you start identifying with your feelings. That's when you start talking like this:

I feel so . . .

    guilty

    ashamed

    worthless

    unloved

    weak

hopeless

ugly

lost

Soon enough your feelings can consume you to the point of your feelings becoming your own personal identity like this:

I *am* dirty and so sinful.

I *am* unpopular and no one likes me.

I *am* that unloved, lonely loser.

I *am* so weak and hopeless that I *am* lost.

It's at this point that your feelings become your new reality and your personal identity. They start to define who you are.

In my observation, it's different for every one of you. Some of you struggle with your personal image. Some of you struggle with guilt. Some of you struggle with anxiety and depression. Some of you struggle with loneliness because your homelife is a mess. Surely some of you face several of these identity issues at the same time, and I know that some of them come and go in different phases of your teen years.

Regardless, your own personal identity becomes the underlying issue for nearly every decision you make. Think about it . . .

How you pose, the filters you use, your best captions, and what you post are all part of carefully crafting your social image and identity online. The same is true with how you react to other people's pictures and stories and how you feel about being in those pictures (or not).

How you look at the rich and famous and beautiful celebrities and wish you could be that rich or famous or beautiful—that has to do with your personal image and identity.

How you freak out about test scores and ACT and AP results has a lot to do with whether you view yourself as a success or a failure. For many of you, it is probably also connected to whether you think your parents view you as a success or a failure.

How you decide whether to drink or smoke or fool around or go all the way with the person you're dating— that all has to do with your identity. Are you cool or not cool? Are you hot or not hot? And after the choices you make, are you ashamed or not ashamed? Are you the dirty sinner who's crossed the point of no return?

Whether you realize it or not, most of your teen years are spent trying to figure out the answer to this one question: *Who am I?*

Now why is this such a big deal? Well, it's a big deal because of the even bigger problem that follows. Once you start to buy into these personal identity issues and feelings, you start to lose track of the facts of who you *actually* are. That's what is most dangerous of all, when you start losing track of *who you are in Jesus.*

So I'm going to refine my answer for you to be a little more clear. What is the biggest problem for teens today? ***The problem is teens losing track of their identity in Christ.***

That is what I believe is most dangerous, disastrous, and damaging in the life of a teen today.

An Identity Solution

So there it is. That is what I believe is the biggest challenge and problem for teens. But don't worry, I'm not going to leave you hanging here. I'm not writing this book just to tell you what's wrong. Yes, I want you to understand the problem. But even better, I'm writing to offer you a solution. And here's the best part—it's not *my* solution. Jesus is the one who offers you this solution.

Follow along with me then. We're going to continue on this journey together. First, we will need to establish who you really are, that is, your identity. We will do this by identifying the facts that will give you a good understanding of who you really are, your true identity in Christ. But take careful note of what I said there. *Facts.* We will be looking at real, true, and honest facts to see who you are in Jesus. Then, once that is crystal clear, we will start to apply your identity in Christ to real life situations and feelings.

So read on, my teen friend. A renewed sense of identity awaits!

Chapter 3

Who You Are

We have identified the problem now. Teens today are losing their grasp on their identity in Christ—who they are in Jesus. We got that down. But what does that mean? And more importantly, what's the solution?

Well I have good news and bad news for you. Which do you usually prefer to hear first—the good news or the bad news? I'm not really a good-news-first kind of guy. I don't want the excitement of the good news to be destroyed immediately by the bad news. Then that bad news just sort of sits with me. I'd prefer to hear the bad news first, deal with it, and then move on and live in the happiness of the good news.

In this particular case, I have some really, really good news and some really, really bad news. And I'm writing this book, so I get to be the one to decide which comes first. So I'm going to give you the bad news first. However, this news is so important you actually *need* to hear the bad news first. If you don't know this bad news, then the good news I have to share won't even matter to you. So here we go, brace yourself for the bad news . . .

You Are a Sinner

There it is. I said it. No beating around the bush or candy coating it. You're a teen and you want everyone to "Keep it 100," so that's as 100 as you're going to get. You're a sinner.

It's always amazing to me what lengths we will go to as humans in order to avoid admitting that. Think of that time you got caught by dad or mom and you lied and lied and lied trying to deny, evade, or do anything possible to avoid admitting you did something wrong. That didn't go so well. You did what you did, and it is what it is.

We do this kind of thing to avoid guilt often. For example, there's also the "I'm not so bad" lie. I say "lie" because that's what it is. We're just trying to fool ourselves. We might think things like, "I'm not *that* bad of a person." Or maybe, "Yeah, OK, fine. I know I've done some bad things. But I've also done a lot of good things. I think I've probably even done more good than bad. So I'm not *that* bad."

But just because you play *Call of Duty* but haven't shot someone, or you gossip all the time but don't personally do the things you talk about, or cheat on a couple tests but not all your tests— those things don't make you right in God's sight.

Do you know what God expects of you? Perfection. I'm talking actual, real life "keeping it 100." God wants you to keep 100% of his laws 100% of the time. In the Old Testament,[7] God said this: "Be holy because I, the LORD your God, am holy."[8]

In the New Testament,[9] Jesus said essentially the same thing. Jesus was talking about what God expects of us in his famous Sermon on the Mount, and he summarized it this way: "Be perfect, therefore, as your heavenly Father is perfect."[10]

God demands perfection from every person, including you, in all things and at all times.

Again, we try to evade and avoid the guilty verdict with another lie. "But I'm not as bad as *that* guy. Come on! I'm not a serial

---

[7] The first part of the Bible that points toward Jesus coming.

[8] Leviticus 19:2

[9] The second part of the Bible that talks about how Jesus came and what that means for us.

[10] Matthew 5:48

killer! I'm not Hitler! Give me *some* credit at least!" But God doesn't want you to be "better" than someone else, he wants you to be *perfect*.

"But I at least try pretty hard . . . But I didn't mean to . . . But everyone else was doing it . . . But I'm still young and I'll get more serious about God when I'm older . . . But it's not that big of a deal."

Excuses, excuses, excuses. We all think things like this. We all try to deflect guilt and pass blame. The truth of the matter, though, is that we are guilty as charged. *I* am guilty as charged. So are you. So is everyone.

King David poetically wrote it this way in Psalm 14:

> The LORD looks down from heaven
>> on all mankind
> to see if there are any who understand,
>> any who seek God.
> All have turned away, all have become corrupt;
>> there is no one who does good,
>> not even one.[11]

Of course there are people in this world that do "good" things. However, we are judging these people by worldly standards. We don't know everything a person does. You might read the headline about the athlete who donates a million dollars to help the needy. But what does that athlete do behind closed doors? You might see a classmate who always seems to have it together and apparently always goes to church. But do you know the thoughts that run through her mind or how she talks to her parents?

The point is, good in our eyes is much different than good in God's eyes. God doesn't want mostly, kinda, sorta, at least

---

[11] Psalm 14:2–3

you're better than others good. God wants totally good. Holy. Righteous. Perfect. All the time.

I don't know about you, but that makes me sweat like a freshman at HOCO because I know myself. I know what I've done. I know how I've treated people. I know what I've said. I know what I've thought. I'm nowhere near perfect. In fact, I'm not even in the same solar system as perfect. But neither are you.

That's why the Bible says this: "*All* have sinned and fall short of the glory of God."[12]

Imagine yourself at the rim of the Grand Canyon. Have you been there? I have, and it is intensely impressive. *Miles* wide. Up to a mile deep. It's breathtakingly incredible. Put it on your bucket list!

Now imagine you are standing on one edge of the Grand Canyon, and you want to get to the other side. But instead of driving all the way around, you're just going to run and jump across. You might be gold medal Olympian Simone Biles ready to do a tumbling pass backflip across the chasm. You might be Jordan in his prime or Giannis with his freakishly long legs and strides. You might be a prime athlete, or you might just barely be more athletic than your grandma. It doesn't matter. You ain't gonna make it. You're going to fall short—*WAY* short—to your peril and death.

The same is true spiritually for you, for me, and for every human. We all fall *WAY* short of God's glory, his standard of perfection for us. And just like a leap off the Grand Canyon's edge, it's going to end terribly. The Bible goes on to say, "The wages of sin is death."[13] That's the cost. That's the price to pay. The wages for disobeying and falling short of a holy and perfect God, the cost for any sin in any amount, is death. Not just

---

12 Romans 3:23 (emphasis added)
13 Romans 6:23

physical death, either. Yes, physical death, but also eternal death and separation from God in hell.

And sorry to kick you while you're down, but it's actually even worse than that. Unfortunately, this is actually the way you came into the world—as a sinner. You were born with a natural sinfulness that was passed down from your parents.[14] So that is to say that though you came into this world kicking and screaming and physically alive, you were actually at the same time spiritually dead.[15] From the time you were born, you were separated from God by your natural sinfulness and you have only continued in the way of sin that leads to death.

This is true for all of us, but let that sink into your own heart and brain for a minute. You're a sinner.

I know what you're thinking, "Yikes, bro. You said bad news, but this is horrible news. Like literally *the worst* news possible."

You're right. It is. But like I told you before, you have to know the bad news, yes, even the worst news, before you truly appreciate the good news.

Think of it this way: If you didn't know you had Stage 4 cancer, would you ever take chemotherapy? In fact, would chemotherapy even cross your mind? I don't think you would ever even think about chemo, and certainly not think you needed it, unless you first knew that you have cancer.

The same is true here. When we are talking about our identity—who we are as people—we first have to understand the cancer of sin living within us. We have to be able to say, "I am a sinner. That's who I am. I need help."

---

[14] Psalm 51:5 Surely I was sinful at birth, sinful from the time my mother conceived me.

[15] Ephesians 2:1 As for you, you were dead in your transgressions and sins.

But good news, my friend! You do have help! You made it through the worst news, and now, the best news is yet to come!

You Are a Saint

God is a holy and perfect God. He is fully righteous, and he would be fully just to judge and condemn us. In fact, he wouldn't be a very good or fair judge if he *didn't* punish those who do wrong. Yet God is also a loving and gracious God who doesn't want sinners to die and be separated from him forever in hell. But don't just take my word for it—listen to God himself! "As surely as I live, declares the Sovereign LORD, I take no pleasure in the death of the wicked, but rather that they turn from their ways and live."[16] God doesn't delight in sinners dying. Quite the opposite actually. "[God our Savior] wants all people to be saved and to come to a knowledge of the truth."[17]

This is who our God is—a compassionate, gracious God who loves sinners and wants them to be saved. God even has a special name that tells us so. Did you see that name tucked away in the Ezekiel verse? The special name is LORD in all capital letters. That's the Bible translators' tricky way of telling you that the Hebrew word being used is the name we sometimes say is *Yahweh* (pronounced Yah-Way), or even occasionally Jehovah.[18] It's an awesome name. God himself defined that name Yahweh once for Moses and the Israelites this way:

> The LORD, the LORD, the compassionate and gracious God, slow to anger, abounding in love and faithfulness, maintaining love to thousands, and forgiving wickedness, rebellion and sin.[19]

---

[16] Ezekiel 33:11
[17] 1 Timothy 2:4
[18] How Yahweh turned into Jehovah is a *really* long story. But it did. Ask a fancy-pants, Hebrew-knowing pastor sometime and be mesmerized by his linguistic genius! Besides, who wouldn't want to learn more about word origins instead of watching YouTube? #YesIamnerdy
[19] Exodus 34:6–7

Every single time you see that name LORD in all capital letters, Yahweh, this is what you can think about. Our God is the God who is faithful to himself, to his promises, and to his love. He is compassionate, gracious, patient, loving, and forgiving.

Now if you're paying attention—and I know you aren't listening to music and binging Netflix simultaneously while reading this book—then perhaps some questions come to your mind. "Wait a second! How can this be? Didn't you say God is a righteous and holy judge who punishes sinners? Now you're saying he is a loving and patient God? That sounds kinda whack! That's contradictory! How can God be *both* a righteous judge who punishes *and* a merciful God who loves and forgives *at the same time*? That doesn't make sense!"

Well if that's what you are thinking, you're right. It doesn't jive. It doesn't work. It doesn't make any sense at all.

Except . . .

Except at the cross. I'll explain. Or better, I'll let Jesus himself explain with his own famous words:

> God so loved the world that he gave his one and only Son, that whoever believes in him shall not perish but have eternal life. For God did not send his Son into the world to condemn the world, but to save the world through him.[20]

God is certainly a righteous and holy judge who will condemn sinners. But God is *also* loving and forgiving *at the same time*. That's why he sent his Son Jesus into the world—to make all things right and to fix the problem, to bring a cure for the cancer of sin.

How did Jesus do that? I'm glad you asked!

---

[20] John 3:16–17

The apostle Paul explains it this way:

> God was reconciling the world to himself in Christ, not
> counting people's sins against them . . . God made him
> who had no sin to be sin for us, so that in him we might
> become the righteousness of God.[21]

Imagine a boyfriend and girlfriend in a HUGE fight. (Hard to
imagine, right?) Let's say someone comes along, a third party,
and helps to make the relationship right again. That really nice
and helpful friend brought peace to the fighting couple. The
relationship is now *reconciled*.

That's what Jesus did. He made our relationship with God right
again. But he didn't do it with a dozen roses and a sappy card
from the grocery store. Jesus paid a much higher price than
that—himself. Jesus gave himself as the perfect payment for sin
to make sinners right with God.

So first of all, God demands that we be perfect like he is. But we
cannot, and we have not. Enter Jesus. The life you can't live, he
did. The Bible says, "We have one who has been tempted in
every way, just as we are—yet he did not sin."[22] He was "a lamb
without blemish or defect."[23] This is what we mean when we say
Jesus was *righteous*. God demands perfection and Jesus was
perfect in every way—every thought, every word, every action all
the time.

That's the perfection part of God's demands. But what about
the other part? What about the verses that tell us that sinners
deserve death and punishment? I'm still a sinner and I still have
hell to pay for what I've done—literally. Not to worry! Jesus
took care of that, too!

---

[21] 2 Corinthians 5:19, 21
[22] Hebrews 4:15
[23] 1 Peter 1:19

John the Baptist once saw Jesus, pointed at him and said, "Look, the Lamb of God, who takes away the sin of the world!"[24] Later, a different John (John the disciple) wrote, "The blood of Jesus, his Son, purifies us from all sin."[25] So not only did Jesus live the perfect life that we could not, but he also paid the price we could not. Look at the following beautiful prophecy/promise that God made to his people about 700 years before he sent his Son. Pay careful attention to the contrast in pronouns. I emphasized them to help.

> Surely *he* took up *our* pain
>   and bore our suffering,
> yet we consider him punished by God,
>   stricken by him, and afflicted.
> But *he* was pierced for *our* transgressions,
>   *he* was crushed for *our* iniquities;
> the punishment that brought *us* peace was on *him*,
>   and by *his* wounds *we* are healed.
> *We* all, like sheep, have gone astray,
>   each of us has turned to our own way;
> and the LORD has laid on *him*
>   the iniquity of us all.[26]

Do you see the contrast? Do you see the exchange that took place? That is what Paul was explaining to us in the Corinthians passage on the previous pages. It all happened at the cross. There on Calvary a great exchange took place. All of Jesus' righteousness (his perfection and holiness) came over to us, and all of our sin (our failures, faults, and guilt) went over to him at the cross. At the same time, he paid the debt we owe. He died and paid the wages of sin with his own death. And thus, as Paul says, God no longer counts our sins against us.

---

[24] John 1:29
[25] 1 John 1:7
[26] Isaiah 53:4–6 (emphasis added)

See, I told you it was great news! Really, it's earth-shattering, life-changing, epically amazing news! Just look at how some of the passages we've looked at change once Jesus enters the picture:

> All have sinned and fall short of the glory of God, _and all_
> _are justified freely by his grace through the redemption that came by_
> _Christ Jesus._[27]

> The wages of sin is death, _but the gift of God is eternal life in_
> _Christ Jesus our Lord._[28]

You are a sinner. I am a sinner. We all are sinners who have fallen far short of God's glory and deserve death. But the gracious and undeserved gift of God is life instead of death. Why? Because he justified you (declared you to be innocent) for free by his grace through the payment that Jesus made.

Imagine for a moment an intense courtroom scene. The defendant is standing on trial and is a real scumbag—a dirtball of a person who has done _a lot_ of bad things. The accusing attorney presents all the evidence of past crimes (Did I mention it's _a lot?_). The accused is dead to rights. The death penalty is coming. Yet before the judge slams down his gavel, the defense attorney jumps to action. "Wait!" he says. "Stop! I'll take the sentence. I'll take the punishment. When you think of the defendant, think of my record instead. When you sentence the defendant, sentence me instead." The courtroom falls silent in shock and awe as the judge slams down the gavel and pronounces the final verdict—the defendant, the criminal, is now declared _not_ guilty.

That's what it means to be justified. And that, dear reader, is what has happened to you. No matter how much Satan wants to accuse you of your sins,[29] and there are _a lot_ of sins, the verdict is

---

[27] Romans 3:23–24 (emphasis added)
[28] Romans 6:23
[29] By the way, did you know that _Satan_ means _accuser?_

already in. Yes, *already* in. It's not coming in the future. It's already done. Or as Jesus said on the cross, "It is finished."[30] You have already been declared not guilty for the sake of Jesus Christ in God's eternal courtroom. It's all yours for free, right now, and forever.

This means that you now have a new status before God. You, sinner, are now a saint in God's sight. Don't be fooled though. Some people abuse the word saint and use it to mean someone who is above and beyond good, some Christian who has achieved more than another Christian. Not at all! By biblical definition, a saint is nothing more than a person who has been set apart as holy—someone declared righteous in God's sight. In other words, *you*. By faith in Jesus as Savior, every believer has the status of saint in God's sight.

A New Identity

This new status given to you by Christ means that you also now have a new identity in Christ. God's gracious gift of forgiveness in Jesus gives you a new life. The Bible says: "If anyone is in Christ, the new creation has come: The old has gone, the new is here!"[31] Like Peter Parker who became Spiderman, but *way* better, you have this new life, this new identity in Christ. It's a life where you are free to live and to serve and to love God and others.

Now don't worry and wonder, "How am I ever going to live up to that? How can I do that?" Not only do you have a new life in Jesus, but you have a new life with Jesus living *in you*! Take a look:

> I have been crucified with Christ and I no longer live, but Christ lives in me. The life I now live in the body, I live by faith in the Son of God, who loved me and gave himself for me.[32]

---

[30] John 19:30
[31] 2 Corinthians 5:17
[32] Galatians 2:20

This is actually where the name Christian comes from. It's not only that you follow Christ. Sure, that's true. But it's actually so much more than that. A Christian is someone who identifies with Christ. Christians live for Christ because he lived and died for them, but Christians also have Christ living in them and through them. So in a sense, you, young Christian, are like a little Christ walking around in this world.

That may sound strange or even silly, but it's really so awesome. Think about it. When our great God and Father in heaven—the Maker and Creator of the entire universe—looks at you, he doesn't see your stains and blemishes. He doesn't see your sin, and he doesn't see your guilt. He sees his Son, Jesus Christ. And that special status and identity come to you in a very special way.

Check out these awesome verses:

> Or don't you know that all of us who were baptized into Christ Jesus were baptized into his death? We were therefore buried with him through baptism into death in order that, just as Christ was raised from the dead through the glory of the Father, we too may live a new life.[33]

> In Christ Jesus you are all children of God through faith, for all of you who were baptized into Christ have clothed yourselves with Christ.[34]

> See what great love the Father has lavished on us, that we should be called children of God! And that is what we are![35]

Everything that is you has been wrapped up—clothed—in everything that is Jesus. When God looks at you, he sees his

---

[33] Romans 6:3–4
[34] Galatians 3:26–27
[35] 1 John 3:1

Son; thus, he sees you as his own dear child. These verses, along with others in the Bible, make it clear that this happens to us in baptism. Think of baptism as God's eternal adoption papers.

When a baby is adopted into a family, the child hasn't done anything to get into the family. It's the parents who simply love and welcome the child into a new life and new family. They even give the child a new identity with their own family name. Even if the child later disobeys the parents, goes on a wild sinful streak, or one day questions if they really belong in the family, the status and identity never change. The facts of the adoption and the adoption papers still stand.

God works the same way in baptism. Christians are baptized *in the name of* the Father, Son, and Holy Spirit. God puts his name on you in baptism and gives you a new identity as you are clothed with Christ and his perfect righteousness. You have *his* family name. No matter how you may sin or go astray or even question your status, the fact is that God has adopted you into his family as his own dearly loved child.

One Bible story that continues to rise toward the top of my all-time favorites list is the Transfiguration of Jesus. Do you know that story? Not too long before Jesus went into Jerusalem to suffer and die on Mount Calvary, he ascended a different mountaintop. He took his three closest disciples along with— Peter, James, and John. There Jesus suddenly changed (transfigured) before them to be shining with his true glory as true God. Moses and Elijah even momentarily appeared next to him. But then, the Father spoke from the heavens and said, "This is my Son, whom I love; with him I am well pleased."[36] It's especially cool that these are the exact same words that were spoken by the Father at Jesus' baptism.[37] The Father put his full stamp of approval on his perfect Son whom he loved so dearly. What is unfathomably incredible and a mystery of all time is that God now looks at you in just the same way. You, yes *you*, my

---

[36] Matthew 17:5
[37] Matthew 3:17

dear teen—God looks at you every single day and is so pleased to say to you the same thing he said at Jesus' baptism and transfiguration, "Yes, this one. *This* is my son/my daughter whom I love and with whom I am so pleased."

You might say one more time, "How can this be? What have I done besides sin?" But the answer is still the same. It's all Christ. Christ *for* you, Christ *in* you, Christ *through* you. And that work of Christ is all yours by faith and in baptism.[38]

Building off of that thought of Christ for you, in you, and through you, I want to share with you now what will serve as a sort of theme verse for this book. I find this verse quite mysterious. It's so profoundly mind-blowing that it's hard for human brains even to begin to understand. And yet it's true. Are you ready for it? Here it is:

> For you died, and your life is now hidden with Christ in God.[39]

Old you is gone. Dead as a doornail. You were crucified and buried along with Christ, and you rose to life with Christ just as he emerged triumphant from the tomb. Therefore, your life is now "hidden with Christ in God."

I love that phrase. I struggle to understand that phrase fully, but I love it. I'll do my best to explain what it means for you.

Right now, people don't look at you and say, "Hey look at that awesome teen over there! That person is just like Christ—basically a mini-Jesus here on earth!" First of all, no one says that. Secondly, it might be mildly creepy if they did.

---

[38] By the way, if you have never been baptized, that's OK! But there's no time like the present! Find a pastor who can explain to you the riches of God's grace and forgiveness in baptism and then go for it. This means of grace, baptism, is available to you at any time for the best price ever—free!

[39] Colossians 3:3

But the main reason no one talks like that is because they can't tell. Yes, you may follow God's commands or show love to others as your faith "shines" at times, but really they couldn't know for sure. If you stood side by side with an unbeliever in a lineup, no one would know the difference just by looking at you. Furthermore, your life doesn't magically become special by worldly standards simply because you believe in Jesus. Following Christ doesn't make unicorns carrying gold gallop out of the heavens into your backyard, or even fill your wallet with cash for that matter. Quite the opposite actually. Usually Christians suffer *more* for following Jesus. Thus, you normally can't tell by looking at someone, "Hey, that's a Christian right there!"

In fact, your new life in Christ is so hidden that sometimes it's probably even hard for *you* to tell. You can't look in the mirror and see Jesus' life and death covering over you. You don't hear God erupting in words from the heavens over your bed as you close your eyes in sleep about how much he loves you. And most certainly, you don't always *feel* like a mini-Christ (a Christian).

And yet, you are. That is your status. That is your new identity. You can identify with Christ as a dearly loved child of God. It's just that at this present moment in a world tainted by sin that life is "hidden with Christ in God." But don't worry! God knows your status. Jesus gave it to you. It's solidified and proven in your baptism. And soon enough you'll be in heaven where there will be nothing "hidden" at all about your identity as a mini-Christ.

That leaves us then with one more thing to sort out. Now you know who you are. You are a dearly loved child of God who can identify with Jesus Christ. He is your life, your love, your all. This is your new identity. But this whole "hidden" life thing is tough—*especially* when it comes to feelings.

What happens when I don't feel like a Christian? What about when it doesn't feel like God loves me? What about when I feel unloved . . . guilty . . . worthless . . . sad . . . lonely . . . ugly . . . depressed . . . weak?

This is the problem we will take on next as we close out this first part of the book. Before we start applying your new identity in Jesus to real life situations, we need to understand the important difference between feelings and facts.

Chapter 4

Feelings vs. Facts

Have you heard of the glass bridges in China? In 2016 China opened the world's highest and longest glass bridge in the world. They already had quite a few of these adrenaline junkie attractions, but this one was a real doozy. The bridge hangs over 900 feet above the Grand Canyon of China and is over 1,400 feet long (over a quarter mile!). The buzzworthy part about this bridge, like the others, is that it consists mostly of giant glass panels. Thus, when there aren't thousands and thousands of tourists lined up or packing the bridge, you can stand on the bridge and look straight down to the bottom of the canyon. It's a thrill-seeking, selfie-lover's dream! If you haven't seen some of the glass bridge videos, I give you full permission to set this book down (only for a few minutes!) to see some of the hilarious videos of terrified people unable to cross the bridge.

How would you handle this bridge if you happened to be there? Are you the adventurous type that would run across with no problems or worries? Would you cautiously walk across with a bit of a racing heart? Or would you be terrified and run away as fast as you could?

For a moment, I want you to think about three tourists who have come to one of these glass bridges. The first one is very unsure. He convinced himself he was going to conquer his fear of heights. Previously tall ladders gave him the sweats, so he hoped that something extreme would cure him. He nearly fainted twice while waiting in line, but he was bound and determined. By the time he got to the entrance of the bridge he

43

instantly regretted this choice and almost hurled his breakfast everywhere.

As he started onto the bridge, this guy got down on his stomach like a baby learning to crawl. He started shaking as tears welled up in his eyes like one of those freaked out people in the viral videos. Whatever he actually paid attention to in science classes back in school, he was about to put into practice. He slowly began to army-crawl his way across the bridge, hoping to distribute his weight evenly and prevent the bridge from shattering beneath him.

The second tourist was about 30 people behind him in line. She also had some fear of heights but not quite so bad. She was there with her family and wanted to look tough to them, so she was resolved to go across no matter what. As she approached the entrance, her body suddenly became slightly shaky as she couldn't take her eyes off the bottom of the canyon. As this tourist started out, she tiptoed onto the bridge like a ballerina on stage. She thought if she took gentle, quick steps it would reduce the possibility of her breaking through and falling. Eventually she caught up to the crawling tourist, but she was still going at a turtle's pace.

Then there was the third tourist. Bro was the epitome of an adrenaline junkie. If he was allowed, he would have base or bungee jumped off the bridge right then and there. This guy got to the bridge about 10 minutes after the first tourist and 5 after the second. The two of them were still nervously making their way across. But this third tourist was determined to be *that guy* on the bridge. He ran out onto it. He laid down on the glass on his back and took a selfie with all 900 plus feet beneath him. He got up and ran some more. He jumped up and down just to prove a point (and annoy the other tourists). Quickly he ran past the first two tourists and to the other side.

Eventually, all three of these tourists made it across the glass bridge. Granted, it took the first guy well over an hour, but they all made it. My question is this: What was the difference between each tourist?

When it finally boils down to it, there was one big difference between each—their amount of faith. One had almost no trust in the bridge, the second a fair amount, and the third tourist had a massive amount of trust in the bridge.

Now the crazy thing is that neither of the first two scared tourists, nor any tourist for that matter, needed to be afraid. The glass on the walkway is not like the glass in your bedroom window. The walkway is made of three panes of tempered, reinforced glass totaling about half a foot thick. You can actually find YouTube videos of people slamming on the glass with a sledgehammer and yet no one falls through.

In other words, the bridge was a perfectly solid foundation for the three tourists to put their faith in! There was no need to be afraid! Thankfully, the *fact* of the matter is that bridge was strong enough to spare from death everyone from the terrified doubter (the first tourist) to the pridefully overconfident (the third tourist).

The same is true with our faith. In the last chapter I talked about the picture of us being on one side of the Grand Canyon as sinners and God with his glory on the other side. The awesome thing about the Christian faith is that your bridge to heaven that will save you from falling to your death (not into a canyon but into hell), is rock solid. Jesus Christ is that bridge from death to life. He is the rock-solid foundation that we stand on!

Some days you might feel so afraid that you are filled with doubts. Some days you might feel so guilty that you wonder if God could ever love you. Some days you might feel so helpless and weak that you think you can't possibly carry on. Then again, there might be other days that you feel energized, strong, and enthusiastic about your faith. But you see the thing is, on every one of those days and in every one of those scenarios you are still standing on Christ. He still lived for you. He still died for you. He still rose for you. Those *facts* have not changed and will not change no matter how you feel.

And there it is! Do you see it in that last paragraph? Do you see the difference between the two? Do you see the problem that arises in our hearts? It's the conflict of how you feel versus the facts of what Christ has done. Understanding the difference between feelings and facts and knowing what you're standing on will make all the difference. Thus, we need to take a closer look at feelings and facts.

Be Careful with Your Feelings!

One of the unique ways that God has blessed you beyond any of the creatures in his creation is with your feelings. Animals seem to have instinctual feelings, such as fear when they run away from danger or love and care when they provide for and protect their young. But human feelings are much different. They are connected to your intellect, your reason and logic, and your human will.

For example, a rabbit may have ears that perk up before it bolts out of your yard as you approach because there is instinctual fear. But as a human, you are able to intellectually process and communicate about fear. "Uh uh. No way. Nope. I'm not jumping out of a plane. If something goes wrong I might fall to a terrible death, and that scares me."

OK, TBH, I'm talking about myself here. I think I happen to be a very logical and reasonable person. Thus, I will never ever jump out of an airplane. I don't care what people tell me about the odds or statistics or all the backup parachutes. The way I see it, the thing will either work or it won't work. And in my mind, that means I have a 50/50 chance—I'm either going to live or I'm going to die. You AP math wizards can get off my case. I don't want to hear it. This is the way I see it.

But then again, do you see how *feelings* are affecting my choices? Coupled with my logic and my reason, the *feeling* of fear is severely clouding the *facts* about my sky-diving safety.

One more example of human feelings versus animal feelings. Let's think about love for a moment. A mama bear may instinctually provide for her cubs and protect her cubs.[40] But only human parents can fully understand and grasp the love of a parent for a child. Only a human parent can describe the miracle of conception and childbirth or communicate the priceless value of their child.

Speaking of parenting, consider how animals act on instincts to mate and reproduce. I don't think anyone would say, "Awww! Look how much they love each other!" That's not real love. Not the way we know it and not the way the Bible describes it. Only humans can show self-sacrificing love, a love that chooses to care for another through thick and thin, a love that is committed to a friend or sibling or spouse or child.

The point is, the ability to have feelings and emotions as a human being is a wonderful gift of God. However, like everything else in this world, sin has tarnished this gift, too. Something good that God has given to us can be interfered with when sin enters the picture.

Knowing this, let's get practical now and think about feelings when it comes to faith.

If you are a Christian, I would imagine you have experienced times when your faith is pulsating so fervently that you feel like a Marvel Avenger of Christianity. Maybe an unexpected, incredible blessing came your way and you felt overwhelmed with thanks to God. Maybe you've stood at the foot of a mountain or the shore of an ocean and were filled with awe and wonder for our

---

[40] Talk about fear! The few times I've seen a mama bear I have definitely run or driven away *fast*!

Creator-God. Maybe a pastor's sermon had some truths about Jesus' love and forgiveness that really touched your heart, or you came across a Bible verse that really meant a lot to you and helped you through something tough. Likely in these moments you had very good feelings associated with your faith. You may have felt like a strong Christian.

But beware of your feelings! Living in an imperfect world, you've probably had the opposite experiences, too. Your family gets the unexpected news of a loved one who passed away. Your hopes and dreams are crushed as you are cut from the team or the musical cast. In a moment of reflection, your sins and your guilt begin to overwhelm and crush you. Or using a present example, right now I'm writing this book during the 2020 Coronavirus pandemic. Plenty of people have been crushed by this. Millions of teens had sports, events, prom, graduation, and more ripped away from them.

When we experience these things, suddenly waves of different feelings come crashing down on us. "I feel lost . . . helpless . . . weak . . . ashamed, etc." Or maybe you've even gotten to the point where you've thought, "I feel like I've lost my faith. I feel like I'm not even a Christian anymore."

Do you see how sin disrupts and damages God's good gifts of feelings and emotions? Sin clouds our minds with fear, guilt, worry, anxiety, and other feelings to the point that we obsess about the *feelings* instead of the *facts*.

Consider some biblical examples. There are a ton I could use, but I'll give you just a few:

> Abraham. God gave promises to Abraham about making him into a great nation and about a special promised child to come through him. Yet fear and/or doubt led him to take matters into his own hands often. He slept with his wife's servant Hagar and had a child through her. He also lied not once but twice to foreign leaders

48

about his wife in an attempt to protect her. Fear and doubt led Abraham away from the facts of God's promises.

The Israelites. Where do we even begin with them? Let's go to the Red Sea. God had just sent 10 incredible (and devastating) plagues on Egypt. The Israelites had every reason to be confident in the Lord from his words and promises, as well as his mighty acts and wonders. But as they approached the Red Sea and turned to see Pharaoh's army barreling down on them, they were filled with fear and complained to Moses. Even when God worked an unthinkable miracle to deliver them through the Red Sea, and then countless others over the next 40 years in the desert, they continued to whine and complain. Despite the *facts* of who God is and what he had done, their *feelings* of fear, weakness, and worry clouded their faith and trust in God.

Elijah. Elijah had just been on the winning side of one of the most epic showdowns of all time. God proved his power on Mount Carmel to Elijah and all the prophets of Baal in an unforgettable striking of fire from the heavens. Yet in the very next chapter of the Bible we see a very different Elijah. Wicked Queen Jezebel threatened to kill him and so he ran in fear to the wilderness. There by himself he felt so alone and helpless that he said, "I have had enough, LORD. Take my life."[41] Elijah was dwelling on his *feelings* of fear, helplessness, and despair instead of the *facts* of what God had done and what God had said.

Peter. Think about the time Jesus came to the disciples walking on water. The disciples were so shocked that they thought he was a ghost. When Jesus identified himself, Peter boldly asked if he could walk on the water,

---

[41] 1 Kings 19:4

too. Jesus invited Peter to join him on the water. So Peter had the *facts* of seeing Jesus and his miraculous power walking on the water and the *facts* of what Jesus said (saying he could walk on water, too). Yet as soon Peter felt the wind and saw the waves, *feelings* of fear overcame him and he began to sink.

There are countless other examples in the Bible. However, did you notice among these examples how God gave clear facts to his people? His words were clear. His promises were clear. His acts of power were clear. What more could they want? The facts of their all-powerful, loving, and gracious God were crystal clear. Yet as soon as they started to fixate on their own feelings, everything quickly crumbled.

Quick side note: Did you also notice the underlying feeling for all of these stories? Fear. Fear is a crippling and consuming feeling, and I'm going to suggest to you that it is fear that is behind most of our bad feelings. Think about it:

> When you feel anxious or worried, isn't it because you're afraid of something bad happening?

> When you feel sad or depressed, isn't it at least in part because you're afraid that nothing and no one can give you happiness and joy?

> When you feel weak, isn't it because you're afraid that you can't overcome or get through some trial or trouble?

> When you feel guilty, isn't it because you're afraid that God won't forgive you?

You may not always realize or actively think about it, but, deep down inside, fear is usually the general commanding an evil army of feelings that attack us and our faith.

So be careful with your feelings! In a sinful world filled with sinful people, we will be constantly riding a rollercoaster of emotions. Sometimes we will be riding high, feeling on top of the world and feeling like we have a strong faith. Other times we will plummet to the depths in what seems like a fear-filled free fall, feeling like we have the weakest or worst faith possible.

But take a deep breath, friend. You can learn to overcome the rollercoaster ride of feelings. You can learn to stand on solid ground. You can learn to know who you are without being confused by your feelings. So what do you need to know so that you don't get lost in your feelings?

The facts!

Learn to Stand on the Facts!
For all the many examples of people in the Bible who got lost in their fear-driven feelings, there are also plenty of examples of believers who stood firmly on the facts of who God is, what God says, and what God has done. Let's consider a few.

> Noah. Noah had every reason according to human standards to be overwhelmed by feelings of fear, sadness, loneliness, and more. We can only imagine how the other people of the world roasted him mercilessly when they saw him building an ark bigger than a football field. Yet Noah trusted the Lord and believed his words. He stood firmly on the facts instead of being washed away by the floodwaters of feelings.

> Abraham. Abraham may have had his moments of doubts or worry, but there is a reason he's also listed in the Bible as a hero of faith. There are a number of examples from his life, but I want to focus on one unthinkable test of faith. After finally having the son that God had promised, God asked Abraham to sacrifice Isaac. The amazing thing is that we never hear one hesitation or complaint from Abraham. Not when God

asked him. Not when Isaac started to catch on that they had no animal to sacrifice. Not even as Abraham raised the knife into the air, ready to plunge it down before God finally stopped the test and provided a ram to take Isaac's place.[42] But what is truly remarkable is the commentary we hear later in the book of Hebrews: "Abraham reasoned that God could even raise the dead."[43] In other words, Abraham knew that God had promised this son to him, and he knew that God promised a Savior would come from the family line of that son. Abraham also knew that God couldn't and wouldn't break a promise. So instead of standing on the shaky ground of feelings, Abraham stood firmly on the facts of who God is and what God said. He knew the fact that God would perform a miracle and raise his son from the dead before God would ever break a promise he had made.

David. David surely had his awful moments where his feelings and sinful passions got the best of him. But he also had some remarkable moments of confident faith. Consider his infamous battle against Goliath. It almost seems impossible for a human—a small, untrained, shepherd boy human no less—to stand fearlessly before a literal giant who was a fierce and mighty warrior. Oh, and David had a slingshot and a few stones while Goliath had impressive armor and weapons! Yet David knew the facts. Here's what he said: "You come against me with sword and spear and javelin, but I come against you in the name of the LORD Almighty, the God of the armies of Israel, whom you have defied. All those gathered here will know that it is not by sword or spear that the LORD saves; for the battle is the LORD's, and he will give all of you into our hands."[44] David overcame his

---

[42] A picture, by the way, of the Savior who would come to take our place as the sacrifice for sin.
[43] Hebrews 11:19
[44] 1 Samuel 17:45, 47

feelings and this "giant" problem by faith in the facts about his Savior God.

Paul. There are few people who have suffered for the name of Jesus more in history than the apostle Paul. He was ridiculed, beaten, flogged, stoned, and imprisoned— and all of those things he experienced multiple times over. Feelings of weakness, helplessness, hopelessness, fear, and more could have easily stopped him in his missionary tracks. But Paul wrote regularly in his letters—many of them from prison—about his confidence that God would deliver him. Maybe God would deliver him from his suffering or maybe God would deliver him from this world to heaven. Either way, Paul could say that, "For to me, to live is Christ and to die is gain."[45] Paul had the confidence to "press on toward the goal to win the prize for which God has called me heavenward in Christ Jesus."[46] This confidence came not from his own inner feelings of determination or strength, but from the facts of God's grace in Christ that guaranteed him a life to come in heaven.

There are many other examples in the Bible we could examine. But these few illustrate the point. When Christians stand by faith to overcome problems—be it suffering or struggle or trial or trouble or persecution—they don't put their faith in themselves or in their feelings. That ground is too shaky. That ground isn't reliable. Our feelings are always all over the place. No! Christians stand firmly on the facts of who God is, what God says, and what God has done. Your feelings may change, but God never does!

And when it comes to God and facts, there is one particular fact that ties together everything of who God is, what God says, and what God has done. This one fact brings everything together

---

[45] Philippians 1:21
[46] Philippians 3:14

and changes your life forever. Let's reflect on that one foundational fact for a bit right now.

The Greatest Fact of All

Talk about feelings! Their world had just been flipped upside down. They were reeling from the most painful thing a human can experience—the death of a loved one. But this particular loved one was special. *Really* special. They had hoped, along with many others, that this Jesus was going to change everything for them. But now he was dead.

All of Jesus' followers were devastated by his crucifixion and death. All of Jesus' followers felt confused, afraid, overwhelmed, and hopeless. What were they going to do now?

It was the women who had the courage to do something at least. They got up early on that Sunday morning to go to the tomb to anoint Jesus' dead body with spices. Imagine what was going through their minds as they walked toward the tomb. What would they have said to each other? Would they have discussed all their fears about the coming days and months? Would they have said anything besides discussing how they were going to move that massive stone away?

Then as they approached the tomb, they saw the stone rolled away and an angel of the Lord shining bright like lightning with clothing as white as snow. The Bible says the guards were so afraid they fell to the ground as if they were dead. But the women were overwhelmed by feelings of fear, too. That's when the angel said this: "Do not be afraid, for I know that you are looking for Jesus, who was crucified. He is not here; he has risen, *just as he said.*"[47]

The angel was making clear for the women two important facts:

---

[47] Matthew 28:5–6 (emphasis added)

1) The tomb was now empty! The same Jesus who was crucified had now risen from the dead and is alive!

2) This also happened *just as he said.* Everything happened just as Jesus had been teaching them. More than that, everything happened just as God had been promising for centuries.

These two facts were made clear by Jesus himself later on that first Easter day. Two disciples were walking on the road to a village called Emmaus. They were very confused by everything that had happened, including the reports of the empty tomb. Suddenly Jesus appeared and was walking with them, though they didn't recognize him at first. Jesus scolded them for not believing what was written about him in the Scriptures. So then, "beginning with Moses and all the Prophets, he explained to them what was said in all the Scriptures concerning himself."[48] All of God's promises about a Savior who would come to suffer, die, and rise again in order to bring life and salvation were all fulfilled in Jesus Christ and proven in his resurrection from the dead.

The apostle Paul wrote extensively about Jesus' resurrection, but perhaps nowhere more clearly than in 1 Corinthians 15. Sometimes we call that "The Great Resurrection Chapter" of the Bible. There Paul makes it crystal clear that Jesus is most definitely alive and that he not only appeared to his disciples but also to more than 500 different people before he ascended into heaven. This is not a conspiracy theory. Jesus rising from the dead is a *fact.*

That fact is a critical fact, because Jesus' resurrection means everything to us. Listen to some of the promises that Jesus himself gave to us:

---

48 Luke 24:27

I am the resurrection and the life. The one who believes in me will live, even though they die; and whoever lives by believing in me will never die.[49]

Because I live, you also will live.[50]

Fact A brings Fact B. Fact A is that Jesus rose from the dead. Fact B is that now you will too. Because Jesus rose to life and conquered death, you will rise to life in heaven in victory. The empty tomb and all the eyewitnesses that saw Jesus prove to us that Jesus is now alive. Because of that great fact of his victory, our victory is also a fact that is as good as done. All that's left is for us to say, "Thanks be to God! He gives us the victory through our Lord Jesus Christ."[51]

But now let's take this fact and break it down a bit more. Let's apply this fact to your life very specifically right now.

First, I want you to see again how your identity in Christ is connected to this resurrection fact. What Jesus has done becomes yours specifically by faith and through baptism. Remember that the Bible tells us we are connected with Jesus' death and resurrection and also clothed with Christ in baptism. God puts his "family name" on us in those waters of adoption and looks at us as his dear child, just as he looks at his dearly beloved Son Jesus. Therefore, Jesus' empty tomb is what sealed the deal for your new life and new identity, and baptism and faith connect you to that work of Christ.

That means the following is true based on those facts: Jesus crushed Satan. You crushed Satan. Jesus paid for sin. You are now seen as sin-less. Jesus rose to life. You will rise to life. Jesus is victorious. You are victorious. The fact of the resurrection of

---

[49] John 11:25–26
[50] John 14:19
[51] 1 Corinthians 15:57

Jesus proves who he is, the fact of your baptism connects you to it, and thus the resurrection of Jesus makes you who you are.

Secondly, I want you to think very carefully about how you can build your life on the fact of Jesus' resurrection and your new identity in him. Think again about the roller coaster ride of life and all the feelings that come from being in a sinful world. Sometimes there are great blessings, celebrations, and successes. Sometimes there are great tragedies and trials. But no matter what happens to you—whether you get an A+ or an F, whether you are the star of the team or the musical or get cut, whether you're in a long term dating relationship or haven't dated anyone, whether you get the college scholarship you were hoping for or get denied, whether you have lots of family alive or lots that have passed away—no matter what happens to you, **Jesus still rose from the dead.**

See, you may have lots of *feelings* that come and go over time. But those are not what you stand on, they are not what define you. It is the *facts* of who God is and what God has done and what he has made you to be in Christ that will never ever change. Never. Ever.

There is such incredible comfort in all this. It's actually quite freeing. Nothing depends on you. You don't have to feel like a Christian to be a Christian. You don't have to feel saved to be saved. You don't have to feel strong to be strong. You don't have to feel loved to be loved. Everything takes place outside of you and without you. Jesus takes care of it all because Jesus is your everything. Remember our key theme verse? "Your life is now hidden with Christ in God."[52] Everything that you have and that you are and that you will be is because of Christ and through Christ and in Christ. Awesome!

---

[52] Colossians 3:3

Facts Cause True Feelings

There are some people who really get worked up about this feelings business though. "But I want to feel good about myself and about life and about God. I want to feel like I love God and like God loves me." Here's what I normally say to those people:

> Focus more on the facts and the feelings will come naturally!

Here's what I mean by that. I've already shown you that if you focus on your feelings too much, you will end up losing track of who God is and thus who you are in Jesus. But interestingly, there's an Uno Reverse Card at play here. If you focus more on the facts of who God is and who you are in Jesus, the more you will be filled with incredibly wonderful feelings. Take a look:

> The more you focus on the facts and evidence of how God says he loves you and shows you love through Jesus, the more you will feel loved.

> The more you focus on the facts of God's repeated encouragements not to be afraid or on Jesus' promises to be with you always, the more you will feel courageous, safe, and secure.

> The more you focus on the facts of God's strength shown in creation and in miracles and in the victory at the cross, the less you will feel weak and the more you will feel strong to face your struggles.

> The more you focus on the facts of the perfect life, the bloody cross, and the empty tomb of Jesus, the less you will feel guilty and the more you will feel confident in your forgiveness.

Get the picture? If you want to be filled with feelings of true joy, happiness, and peace, if you want to feel loved and valued and strong, if you want any feeling of any value, then focus on the facts of who God is and what God has done.

Does this mean positive feelings of happiness and joy will flip on like a light switch for you? Does this mean that you only need to think about Jesus and every bad feeling will automatically go away? Does this mean that if you sincerely believe in Jesus but still struggle with feelings and emotions that you are doing something wrong? Absolutely not!

Remember that we still live in a sin-filled world with sin-filled people as we battle our own sinful nature. We may have a new identity in Christ, but we still live "under the cross," so to speak. Life in this world will still be a struggle every day. (Remember that whole "hidden in Christ" thing?) Thus, every day is a new day to wake up and remember, "Christ is risen. I am a dearly loved child of God. Everything of Christ is mine by faith and in baptism." In other words, it will take continual work to refocus on the facts so that feelings of happiness, joy, peace, and the like can remain. Sin may have tarnished the feelings and emotions that God blessed humans with. However, everything is restored and is yours now in Jesus, and that fact is what will bring the greatest feelings ever.

Now What?

Now you know who you are. You are a Christian. You are a mini-Christ. You are God's dear child whom he looks at with all the love and joy as when he looks at his own Son Jesus. You can identify with Christ. That is your identity. That's who you are.

Now you also know that your identity is established on facts, not feelings. Feelings deceive us. They come and go. They rise and fall. They are tainted by sin. But the facts of Christ never change. "Jesus Christ is the same yesterday and today and forever."[53] Who Jesus is and what he has done are facts; thus, who you are and the solid ground you stand on are also facts.

---

[53] Hebrews 13:8

But life isn't always that simple, is it? Satan is ruthless and relentless. He's always prowling around like a roaring lion, looking for someone like you to devour.[54] That means you will still have struggles. You'll still face temptations. You'll still fall into those temptations and sin. You'll still have feelings that overwhelm you and your heart and mind will still try and latch onto those feelings instead of the facts.

That's what Part 2 of this book is all about. We're going to take a look at some specific life examples—the kind of stuff that you and your friends go through in teen life. As we look at various stories and examples, we'll first examine the feelings that overwhelm us, but then we'll turn to the facts that comfort us. This is the part where we apply what we have learned about your new identity to real life.

So keep reading! It's about to get real . . .

---

[54] 1 Peter 5:8

Part 2:
Applying Your Identity

Chapter 5

Feeling: I Feel Unloved

vs.

Fact: I Am Loved

The first time Lydia felt it was around kindergarten. At least that's what she could piece together. Vaguely she remembered having her big dance recital and feeling an empty "yucky" feeling in her stomach. She was dolled-up like a princess on stage, but as she looked out into the crowd, dad was nowhere to be found. There were *plenty* of other times before the big recital that this happened. This was just the first she could remember.

There were plenty of other times to come, too. Her first elementary school basketball game and her last middle school basketball tournament. The spelling bee. Eighth grade graduation. Her first HOCO dance. They were all united by one common theme—dad wasn't around.

When Lydia was younger it just seemed weird that dad had a "different" schedule than mom. All she knew was that they were always fighting and always yelling—both at each other and at her. Headphones were the best gift she got in fifth grade because she could hide in her room and listen to music to avoid the mess. Finally in seventh grade was when her parents sat her down to give her the rock-your-world news. "Lydia, we're going to get a divorce." Lydia cried for days after that.

By the end of eighth grade, Lydia had been asking so many questions that mom finally let the info slip—dad had been cheating on mom for years before the divorce. He left her for this other woman. That's why he was never around. As if family life hadn't already been tough, Lydia was crushed.

Little did she know, everything Lydia did was affected by this family environment. She was boy *crazy*. Like Joaquin Phoenix as the Joker crazy. She flirted endlessly. She dressed edgy—just enough to catch all the guys attention. She basically spent all night DMing almost a dozen different guys.

Yet all the hard work didn't seem to pay off. Freshman year three guys dated and dumped her, and no relationship lasted longer than a few weeks. Sophomore year she really fell for a guy. They were super serious for about five months, but then he started acting like a real "bro." Typical high school guy. Nice when they were alone, but a jerk when he was with his friends. He constantly made fun of Lydia, even throwing in a couple jokes about her dad on occasion. After a year of messy dating, the relationship finally crashed and burned.

Now that she was finally starting to understand everything she had experienced in life, it hurt *so much* to take it all in. The one person who was supposed to love her and provide for her and the family, her dad, was never there and completely failed her. Her mom tried her best to hold everything together. But because she wanted Lydia to have so many good things, her mom was super demanding and all up in her business all the time.

Then the most painful thought finally struck Lydia's mind. She had *never* seen what real love is like. Never seen it. Never experienced it. Never felt it. And to her terror, she realized she didn't know how to show it, either. How would she know what to look for in a guy when she never saw anything worthwhile from dad? How would she know how to show love and affection if every relationship she had seen or been in had crumbled to pieces? How would she ever find the love of her life to marry someday if she had no clue what a real marriage was supposed to be like?

By this time Lydia was close to finishing her junior year. She was already looking at colleges and thinking about her career and her future. But it was *so* difficult to concentrate on any of that important stuff because the older she got, the more she became overwhelmed with this one consuming thought—*I feel so unloved.*

Feeling Unloved

There isn't much pain one can experience in life that hurts more than feeling unloved. You can handle the ups and downs of growing up if you feel loved and supported by your parents. You can get through little arguments in a relationship if you feel that you are still loved by that other person. You can bear bad news if you feel loved and encouraged by your friends. But if you don't . . . ouch!

Even in a perfect world free from sin, God knew that it wasn't good for humans to be alone.[55] That's why he created Eve for Adam. That's why he instituted marriage and why most marriages are blessed with children. God created humans to know harmony and unity in perfect love, and our perfect love with each other would imitate his perfect love for us. The husband loving a wife would imitate God's selfless, protecting, and providing love for us. Parents loving their children would imitate how our heavenly Father loves us as his children. Friends loving each other would imitate the companionship and harmony we have as the created with our Creator God. It was a profoundly perfect design. An entire world of people would love each other, and each relationship would be a reflection of God's great love for us.

But sin ruined all of that.

---

[55] Genesis 2:18

Oh sure, love is still in the world. And God most definitely loves us (I'll get to that more in a minute). But our love in this world has been tarnished. Sin makes our love for each other and for God far less than perfect. Sin causes loving relationships to fall apart. And sadly, sin causes the opposite of love as well—hate.

To understand just how much sin has tainted and tarnished love in this world, we need to work toward a better understanding of love. First let's note how our English language dulls and diminishes the word love in our culture. Think about how we use that special word in so many different and not special ways. In any given day I might say, "I love football. I love reading. I love my iPhone. I love music. I love Subway subs and pizza. I love my students. I love my friends, my children, and my wife." While those are all true statements, it is most certainly *not* true that I love all the same equally. It would be an insult to my wife and children to say that I love my phone or Subway subs the same as I love them.[56] It would even be bad for me to love my friends the same way I love my wife and kids. Sorry to my awesome friends, but my wife is WAY better (and cuter)!

In the ancient world there wasn't as much confusion about love as we have in the English world today. In the Greek language, they actually had four different words to express the different types of love that we experience in our lives. In order to understand love better, we will look at these four different types of love as well as the ways that sin has tarnished each one.[57] Here they are:

> *Storge.* (pronounced store-gay) This kind of love could be simply called affection. It's the kind of love that you

---

[56] Even though Subway is delicious! I worked there over 10 years and never got sick of the food once!

[57] Big shout out also to C. S. Lewis here who wrote a book about this called *The Four Loves*. You probably know Lewis from the famous *The Chronicles of Narnia* series. Do yourself a favor and challenge yourself sometime. Put down your phone and do some reading of Lewis' works. He's one of the greatest English writing Christian authors ever.

experience often in life. Perhaps it is simplest to think of *storge* love as the love that you have for your family. How parents and children love each other, or siblings, or cousins, or other close, family-like relationships—these are all examples of this kind of love. Note how this sort of love and affection is very important to us as human beings. The love we receive from our parents and from our siblings was intended by God to model and shadow the way he loves us as our heavenly Father and the way we love each other as a family of believers. With such close relationships, it certainly hurts when sin interferes. You could say that these kinds of people have the number one priority and obligation to love us. Dads and moms and siblings are supposed to love us. We expect that. Thus, when sin gets in the way, and you don't feel loved by those people, it is very painful!

Philia. (pronounced fi-lee-ah) In its most basic understanding, *philia* love is love among friends. Friends are certainly important to us today, but I think we have lost something on this whole friendship business over time. This is another word we have watered down. Now you can "friend" and "unfriend" people online with a quick click. Now the meat and potatoes of your quality friendship with someone might be nothing more than playing online video games for hours together, gossiping about boys, or exchanging a bunch of memes and emojis. That's not real friendship. True friendship is a companionship among people who have similar interests, a desire to be around one another, an ability to be chill even if you haven't seen each other for a while, and a commitment to have each other's backs. As a teen, you certainly understand how important it is to have quality friends in your life. I would bet a lot of money that you have had friend trauma and drama—friend groups changing, lost friends, friends who hurt you deeply. I would also bet that your closest friends are very special people to you. Thus, when sin interferes and ruins friendships, it can be a very traumatic and painful thing—especially for teenagers who rely so heavily on friends!

Eros. (pronounced air-os) Think of *eros* love as passion. Now in and of itself, there is nothing wrong with passion. We often talk about having "passions" for various activities or hobbies in life. It can also be good to have passion for other people. Think of the scene of a new couple dancing at HOCO for the first time, with sweaty palms and racing hearts. That's an example of *eros* love. Or think of the person who posts a monthiversary pic and says, "O-M-Goodness! This has been the best four months of my entire life! I would like totally die without him!" (Spoken in valley girl voice, of course.) That is total *eros* love. God gifted us this type of love to be the height of passionate feelings for each other. In its greatest display, sex between husband and wife would be the ideal expression of this kind of passionate love. However, sin can corrupt this type of love quickly, too. Very often good passionate feelings can turn into lustful passion or selfish passion. Maybe it's easiest to think of it like this—any kind of lusting or sexual sin, or any time a person is acting selfishly in a relationship, usually can be attributed to *eros* love gone wrong.

Agape. (pronounced ah-gah-pay) This is the greatest type of love, or perhaps better said, this is love to its fullest. *Agape* love is self-sacrificing, selfless love. *Agape* love is when you love someone despite who they are or what they have done. It's a love that puts others before yourself. *Agape* is the word that is used in the Bible for the way that God loves us. His love is full of grace and mercy and forgiveness. His selfless love had the best intentions for us as he created this world and put humans in charge of it, and his selfless love is epitomized in the self-sacrificing love of Jesus at the cross. God's intention was that we would enjoy *agape* love with each other. Each of us would put God first in our hearts, and each of us would put others before ourselves. The greatest human example of this is within a marriage. The Bible even uses that word for love, *agape*, as it describes how husband and wife are to love each other.[58] It's probably obvious to you how greatly sin has interfered with *agape* love. You don't have to look far to see people act selfishly instead of selflessly, or in anger instead of patience, or in revenge instead of forgiveness, and so on.

All four of these types of love are wonderful gifts of God. If you have family-type love, friendship-type love, passionate-type love, and selfless-type love in your life, it's a beautiful thing. God designed for you to receive those from your parents, family, friends, and later your spouse. He also designed for you to be able to share those types of love. What a full and meaningful life to be loved and to love others in such rich and full ways!

Sadly, you know full well that our lives are rarely so fulfilling. In fact, I could almost guarantee that in some way, shape, or form you have experienced a LOT of hurt and pain when it comes to love in your life. Why can I be so confident of this?

First of all, in America over 50% of marriages end in separation or divorce. Simply put, that means that likely half of you reading this book have seen your parents' marriage fall apart. And in my experience dealing with countless families over the years, I have never ever seen a divorce where it did *not* cause significant damage, pain, and hurt for the children.

On top of that, the number of children who are born *outside* of marriage continues to skyrocket through the decades. That means that many of you teens either never saw a marriage growing up, or were raised by a single parent, or were raised with

---

[58] See Ephesians 5:21–33.

one parent not in the picture at all. Maybe you even experienced all three of those things.

If you add those two paragraphs together, that means that in the current state of things in America, the odds are *extremely* high that right now you don't have your biological dad and mom together in your home. And even if you do, surely not all married couples are treating each other with Christ-like love!

This hurts! The very people that God designed and intended to love each other selflessly until "death do they part" are the very people that God also designed and intended to love *you* selflessly every step of the way. Together dad and mom are to provide for you and support you and encourage you (yes, even discipline you) as they raise and train you for adulthood. They are to be your first experiences and examples of *agape* love (and also *storge*-affection and *philia*-friendship). They are to be your first and best example of the way that God loves you. When the love of dad and/or mom fails you, it *hurts*. A *lot*.

But sin surely doesn't ruin families only, and I know that you know that, too. How do I know this? Because I see the damage that sin does every single day among teenagers.

Sin leads people to say mean things about the way that you look or dress. It leads people to be completely ugly with their comments on your social media and to spread gossip (true and not true) all over school. It leads people to make you into that viral meme. Sin is why your friends seemed to ditch you for another friend group and now talk trash about you. Sin is why you only yell at and fight with your boyfriend or girlfriend all the time. Sin is why the *philia* love you thought you had with friends seems to crumble and why the *eros* passionate love you had for your boyfriend/girlfriend never turns into selfless *agape* love.

Add up enough of these love failings—at home, with friends, in dating—and it doesn't take long for the devil to feast on your hurting heart like a lion pouncing on easy prey. Satan will whisper in your ear about what an awful person you are and how awful everyone else is and that no one would want you or care about you. Soon enough you become fixated on this one horrible feeling—*I feel so unloved!*

When I feel like this, I need something different. I need some facts . . .

Fact: You Are Loved

It must have been a strange thing, both to see and experience. Here was this person that everyone respected and admired so much. People loved him. Thousands upon thousands flocked to him like teen girls to Harry Styles. He had authority and wisdom. He had power. Lots of power. The things they had seen him do were nearly indescribable. What wasn't there to love about him?

Now they watched this mighty miracle man as he wrapped his outer garment around his waist and stooped down to wash their feet. Dirty, dusty, smelly feet. A servant's job, the job no one wanted to do. But here was Jesus, washing their feet.

In the introduction to this story in the Bible, the disciple John wrote these words: "Having loved his own who were in the world, he loved them to the end."[59] John was so right.

The day was Maundy Thursday, and it was the evening meal (the Passover Last Supper) on the night before Jesus was crucified. As true God, Jesus knew everything that was about to happen. He knew how unloved he would be in the coming hours. A disciple-friend would betray him. The rest of his friends would desert him. His own Jewish people would arrest and accuse him. He would be spit on, beaten, and bloodied by Roman strangers. He would be crucified and then mocked and taunted. And all the while, he the innocent One would carry the sin and guilt of a world of people who did not love him to the fullest.

---

[59] John 13:1

Yet instead of running away or responding in revenge, or even ditching his disciples who just didn't get it, he took time to show them this extreme example of selfless *agape* love. However, washing feet was only the tip of a mammoth-sized love iceberg. Jesus was indeed about to love them to the end—all the way to the end of his life as he died on the cross. There he would not wash feet with water but rather wash away the sins of the whole world with his own blood.

Jesus foreshadowed this boundless love that same night shortly after the meal they shared. Jesus said this:

> As the Father has loved me, so have I loved you. Now remain in my love. I have told you this so that my joy may be in you and that your joy may be complete. My command is this: Love each other as I have loved you. Greater love has no one than this: to lay down one's life for one's friends.[60]

Want to guess what is the Greek word for love in that paragraph? That's right, *agape*. The completely perfect and selfless love that God the Father has for God the Son is the exact same perfect, selfless love that Jesus has shown to you. Jesus wants nothing more than for you to be filled with joy as you remain in and experience his *agape* love that has loved you despite who you are and what you have done.

Sometimes John, the disciple who recorded those words of Jesus, is called the apostle of love. It was a major theme in his writing, as if he wanted us to clearly understand how great God's *agape* love for us is in Jesus. John is the one who wrote these famous verses (all about *agape* love):

> For God so loved the world that he gave his one and only Son, that whoever believes in him shall not perish but have eternal life.[61]

---

[60] John 15:9, 11–13
[61] John 3:16

This is how we know what love is: Jesus Christ laid down his life for us.[62]

God is love.[63]

Our God is so filled with *agape* love that it defines who he is and what he does. He *agape*-loved the world so much that he sent Jesus to love us with a literal self-sacrificing love. His death for us, the sinless on the cross for sinners, is how we know what *agape* love is and how we know that we are loved. That leads us to the first fact to consider in this chapter.

> **Fact #1** – You *are loved!* You know with absolute certainty that you are loved with an endless *agape* love. God sent Jesus for *you.* Jesus died for *you.* You are loved!

Now it's one thing for you to show love for someone you are expected to love. You show love for your boyfriend or girlfriend when you go out of your way to go to one of their games or events or when you buy a thoughtful gift for them. But you're kind of expected to do that. You show love for your parents when you finally realize how many countless hours and dollars they have invested into you, and you do something nice for them in return. That's expected in some ways, too. Though sin interferes, it's normal for people to love family, friends, boyfriend/girlfriend, etc.

However, it's a completely different story when you talk about loving someone who does *not* deserve it. We live in a world where it's normal to treat people in the way they "deserve." Bad breakups end in ghosting someone and broken hearts lead to mean words and revenge posts and people making it clear to their enemies, "You're dead to me." You almost never hear about someone doing something for people that don't deserve it—especially not loving them or even dying for them. But Jesus

---

[62] 1 John 3:16
[63] 1 John 4:16

did. He sacrificed himself in *agape* love for everyone, the worst of sinners included—you included.

Take a look at these beautiful passages that highlight this:

> This is how God showed his love among us: He sent his one and only Son into the world that we might live through him. This is love: not that we loved God, but that he loved us and sent his Son as an atoning sacrifice for our sins. And so we know and rely on the love God has for us. God is love. Whoever lives in love lives in God, and God in them.[64]

> You see, at just the right time, when we were still powerless, Christ died for the ungodly. Very rarely will anyone die for a righteous person, though for a good person someone might possibly dare to die. But God demonstrates his own love for us in this: While we were still sinners, Christ died for us.[65]

This is the definition of *agape* love! It's self-sacrificing and acts in the interests of others, even when they don't deserve it. In the Bible, this is also what is called *grace*. Simply put, grace is *undeserved love*. Sometimes people use an acronym to define it further. Grace is God's Riches At Christ's Expense (G-R-A-C-E). All of the riches of God's love come to you at the expense of Jesus' suffering and death on the cross.

God's love is not self*ish*. It's self*less*. God doesn't demand payment, but made the payment himself. God doesn't expect anything of you, he simply gives everything to you. He joyfully gives you his love freely and fully in Jesus. Always. That amazing news leads us to our second fact to consider:

> **Fact #2** – You are loved *by grace*. Not only is it a fact
> · that God loves you, a fact proven by Jesus' life and death

---

[64] 1 John 4:9–10, 16
[65] Romans 5:6–8

for you, but God also loves you freely and fully. This fact is proven in that, though you don't deserve it, he gives you his love without asking or demanding anything from you first.

Even though we have this gracious love of our God, Satan will still try to trip you up with endless questions. We are used to love being finite—there's an end to it. Usually there is a line people cross where they stop loving. Finally, you can't take how your relationship is going, and you have to break up. Finally, a husband or wife decides that they are done loving their spouse after years of emotional abuse. Finally, that friend has stabbed you in the back so much that you cut them out of your life. As we are used to love ending, Satan might lead us to wonder things like:

> OK, God's love is great. I'm thankful for it. But will he ever stop loving me? What if I sin too much? What if he doesn't care anymore? Will this love ever run out?

Don't listen to the twisting lies of the devil! The answer to all those questions is a resounding NO! But don't just trust me. Trust the facts. Look at this beautiful section of Scripture:

> The LORD is compassionate and gracious,
>> slow to anger, abounding in love.
> He will not always accuse,
>> nor will he harbor his anger forever;
> he does not treat us as our sins deserve
>> or repay us according to our iniquities.
> For as high as the heavens are above the earth,
>> so great is his love for those who fear him;
> as far as the east is from the west,
>> so far has he removed our transgressions from us.
> As a father has compassion on his children,
>> so the LORD has compassion on those who fear
>> him.[66]

---

[66] Psalm 103:8–13

Ever stop to think how high the heavens are above the earth? In a universe that we haven't even begun to fully explore, you could say the heavens extend limitlessly above the earth. That's how great God's love is for you!

Ever stop to think how far the east is from the west? If you drew lines from one point going in opposite directions, the lines would never end in this sprawling universe. That's how far God has removed your sins from you!

God's compassionate, gracious, forgiving love for you is boundless and endless. Rather than trying to figure out if God's love could ever end, focus your attention on trying "to grasp how wide and long and high and deep is the love of Christ."[67] This leads us to a third fact:

> **Fact #3** – You are loved by grace *with a boundless love.* God's gracious love for you is beyond what anyone could ever measure. Instead of wondering if it could ever end, enjoy the fact of the endless tidal wave of his grace!

Satan is relentless, though. So many facts about God's love are clear to us in Jesus and in the words of the Bible. But the devil won't quit yet. He'll throw one more curveball at you, hoping that you will swing and miss with feelings of being unloved.

Just as you are starting to bask in the riches of God's love, you might lose your job. Or wars will break out. Or a pandemic brings the world to its knees. Or protests lead to dangerous riots in your hometown. As I've mentioned before, I'm writing this at a time when our country is reeling from the COVID-19 Coronavirus pandemic and there are violent riots taking place across the country after the death of George Floyd. The amount of frustration, anger, hatred, and general lack of love in our country and on social media right now is nearly unfathomable (except that we expect this in a sin-filled world).

---

[67] Ephesians 3:18

These are the times when Satan strikes with his tempting bait, trying to lure you in: God's gracious, endless love is wonderful. BUT . . . what if something else in this world takes me away from that love?

Don't bite this tempting fruit! That cannot and that will not happen. Look at the following moving words of the apostle Paul. Really take your time with these verses. Immerse yourself in every purely precious word. Maybe even memorize them. Take them to heart and treasure them! Enjoy:

> Who shall separate us from the love of Christ? Shall trouble or hardship or persecution or famine or nakedness or danger or sword? As it is written:
>
>> "For your sake we face death all day long;
>> we are considered as sheep to be slaughtered."
>
> No, in all these things we are more than conquerors through him who loved us. For I am convinced that neither death nor life, neither angels nor demons, neither the present nor the future, nor any powers, neither height nor depth, nor anything else in all creation, will be able to separate us from the love of God that is in Christ Jesus our Lord.[68]

Wow! Speechless. It's hard to know what to say in response to that. Sometimes it's even hard to make it through those words without tears in the eyes. There is so much suffering and sorrow in this world, so much trouble and turmoil, so much danger and disaster. But nothing, not even death itself, can *ever* separate us from the love of God that comes to us in Jesus Christ. Nothing. Ever. That brings us to our final fact:

> **Fact #4** – You are loved by grace with a boundless love that *nothing can ever separate you from*. You are in fact a

---

[68] Romans 8:35–39

conqueror in any and all things because God's *agape* love will always be with you.

Summary

God designed for us to experience love in such fulfilling and beautiful ways—affection, friendship, passion, and selfless love. Every relationship in this world was meant to be filled with love—others loving us and us loving others—all as a shadow of the great love that God has for us.

But sin has interfered with that. While we still experience love, it has significantly tarnished and tainted our love. Far too often we personally experience this as sinful people fail us. When we experience love that fails, it hurts a lot. It hurts when parents fail you. It hurts when teachers fail you. It hurts when your boyfriend or girlfriend fails you. It hurts when friends fail you. These experiences are enough to make us *feel* unloved. But since we have a new life and identity in Christ, we can focus on the *facts* instead. Let's review some of the facts of this chapter:

> Fact #1 – You are loved by God.

> Fact #2 – You are loved by God by grace—freely and fully.

> Fact #3 – You are loved by God by grace with a measureless, boundless, endless love.

> Fact #4 – You are loved by God by grace with a boundless love, and nothing can ever separate you from it.

All of those facts are proven, guaranteed, and yours in Jesus Christ. This is part of your new identity in him. As the Father loves his Son Jesus, so he loves you. No need to doubt or worry. His love is yours now and forever.

Speaking of forever, I want to start drawing your attention away from a sin-filled world to a time and place in which love will be experienced to the fullest—heaven. John, this apostle of love, also wrote the last book of the Bible called Revelation. There he recorded what he saw and heard regarding the times to come and eternity in heaven. Listen to some of the opening words John wrote in Revelation:

> To him who loves us and has freed us from our sins by his blood, and has made us to be a kingdom and priests to serve his God and Father—to him be glory and power for ever and ever! Amen.[69]

Amen indeed!

Want to guess which word for love is used here again? Yup. *Agape*. Because of Jesus' selfless and self-sacrificing love, we have been freed. We have been freed from sin. We have been freed from the dismal life in a world where love fails because of sin. We have been freed from the doom of death. God has brought us into his kingdom to know his *agape* love and to experience his *agape* love and to reflect his *agape* love to others. That love is all yours through Jesus. That's your new identity in him—*agape*-loved child of God. It's all yours in him, now and forever.

Dear teen, trust the facts. Trust God's words.

You *are* loved!

---

[69] Revelation 1:5–6

Chapter 6

Feeling: I Feel Guilty

vs.

Fact: I Am Innocent

Ashley struggled to make eye contact with anyone. Her eyes darted away from her parents, but they thought she was just doing the addicted-to-my-screen thing. At the lunch table her eyes were glued to her food and not her friends as she mustered out a few words of conversation here and there. At church Ashely couldn't manage to look at the pastor during the sermon, but rather fixated her eyes on the service folder or the floor the entire time. Deep down inside she knew that just the right look from just the right person could crush her and lead to a total breakdown.

Then it finally happened.

Ashley was volunteering with some other teens to set up Christmas decorations at church. She was on manger duty with the younger pastor whose main responsibility was serving the teens and families of the church.

"How have you been, Ashley? I haven't seen you in like forever!" he said.

"Umm. OK, I guess," Ashley responded in a voice that did not at all sound OK.

The pastor did his pastor thing. He made small talk, gradually asking deeper questions to see how Ashley really was doing. Then they got onto the topic of her boyfriend. Ashley's voice trembled a bit as she mentioned that they had been having some troubles. The pastor listened and looked at her with every bit of godly compassion.

Then it happened. Eye contact. Ashley immediately burst into tears.

The pastor knew where this was going. He had worked with enough teens. He had known Ashley long enough to know she was acting weird. He had seen her during his last sermon, which happened to be about Jesus and the Samaritan woman at the well who had not been living a very pure life. Ashley was squirming in her seat the whole time. "It's OK, Ashley. If you would like to tell me something, you can." More tears.

Finally Ashley found the courage to choke out some words. "My boyfriend . . . My boyfriend and I . . . we . . . we haven't been so good . . . we . . . we slept together. Three times."

The weeping and wailing that followed sounded like that of a newborn baby. This was ugly crying.

"I just don't know what to do," she said. "I like him so much. But I know it's wrong. It wasn't always like this. But one time we were together, and one thing led to another thing. And then another time it went further. I guess we kinda figured like we had done this, so we might as well do that. It felt like there was no turning back. Then we finally went all the way. I felt *so* terrible, worse than I have ever felt before. That night I threw up twice in my bathroom and didn't sleep the entire night. But somehow we've done it again. He's such a special person, but this is so wrong, and it's like I'm trapped and I can't get out. I feel uncomfortable around my parents. I feel horrible when I'm at church. I feel so ashamed, Pastor. I'm disgusted with myself. I feel so dirty. *I feel so guilty.*"

Feeling Guilty

When you feel guilty, it can be an absolutely sickening experience. Like heart racing, tossing and turning at night, I'm gonna hurl my McDonald's everywhere kind of sick. Have you felt this before?

I know you have. I know this because God has placed into every single human being something very special and important called a "conscience." The conscience is why people all over the world know you don't just walk up to somebody and go, "Hulk smash!" on their face. The conscience is why you could be in Asia or Africa or America and people know you shouldn't kill someone, steal from them, or any number of other things. Yes, because of sin in this world, people still do these things with consciences that are corrupted or corroded. But generally speaking, people have both a natural sense of right and wrong and a learned sense of right and wrong from their parents, their friends, their culture, or the Bible that guides them.

So I know you have a conscience. And I know your conscience works. What have you done that has made your conscience put your whole brain and body on red alert? Or maybe a better question: What is it that's eating at you right now? What makes you feel guilty?

Experience has shown me—including my own personal life—that every person struggles mightily with certain sins. I'm not sure I've met a Christian who struggles with every single sin ever. Rather, one might refrain from sexual temptations but be really weak with bad language. Another might be a very honest student or employee but gives in to peer pressure to drink and do drugs.

What sins are your weakness? Be aware! Watch out! Satan wants nothing more than to lure you with his tempting bait and reel you into that sin. Then, Satan the accuser will work overtime to make you feel so guilty. He wants nothing more than to throw

83

your sins back in your face. And unfortunately, dear teen, your work is harder than ever before!

There has always been sin in this world, and teens have always fallen into sin easily as they struggle through growing up and into Christian maturity. However, it is my opinion that these days it has never been so hard for teens. There has never been a time in history when teens can find themselves deep into sin so easily and so fast.

In a matter of seconds and only a few clicks, millions of XXX pictures and videos could be at your fingertips. Respond to a Snapchat, and you could be meeting up at the designated spot to have marijuana brownies in less than five minutes. Text your plug and then get back to your group chat and coordinate who's bringing what alcohol to the party. Vapes and Juuls can be snuck anywhere in pockets and purses. Gossip can be spread schoolwide in milliseconds. Cheating is as convenient as a click and a scroll on your Apple Watch.[70]

But I don't have to tell you. You're the teen. You know. So I'll come back to my question. What sins do you struggle with? What has been firing up your conscience like coals on a campfire and making you feel so guilty?

> Do you struggle with bad language? Do swear words fly off your lips as fast as the most popular rappers? Is your online video game playing and chatroom filled with vulgarity? Has cussing become just another way for you to express yourself?

> Do you wrestle with cheating? Maybe you have all the teachers fooled about "what a good student you are." But really you have been manipulating Google Docs and using your phone and smart watch like you're the next

---

[70] I have personally worked with teens who have done specifically all of these things, and sadly much more.

Mark Zuckerberg or Jeff Bezos. Maybe for you it's even hard to remember the last time you had an honest grade from your own personal work.

Is your attitude something special? And by special I mean of course nothing special at all. The only thing that's special about it is how incredibly rude you can be to your parents and your teachers. You've become an artist of attitude, manipulating mean words and shooting off sarcasm. You throw shade like it's a solar eclipse. Maybe you've been so busy giving attitude that you barely remember what it's like to be kind to someone.

Have you been caught up in lust? After all, it's everywhere. Your music, TV, movies, the internet. Everyone's talking about sexual things. Maybe you're caught up in the trap of pornography and no matter how hard you try to snap out of it, you keep going back to it. Maybe you've toed the line of purity with your boyfriend or girlfriend, or gone all the way past the line so that now you feel like there's no turning back. It is what it is, and you've done what you've done. You can't unsee the porn or the sext. You can't undo what you did. Maybe you feel like you might as well keep going in such sexual sins.

Are you a party animal? Alcohol. Smoking. Pills. Whatever. You're down for it all. Maybe it started with something small—just a little sip at a party, just one puff when you were alone with friends. But now you're hooked, and it's hard to think of a good time without all this "fun" stuff. Besides, who wants to be the loser sitting at home? This is what your friends do, so why not you too?

Do any of those sins press a button for you? Did any of those trigger your conscience and make you feel a bit uneasy or uncomfortable? Maybe they made you think about other sins I didn't mention but that you struggle with, and now your heart is racing like a NASCAR star. That's your conscience. Look out! Guilty feelings are surfacing!

I have worked with teens that have done all of those things and so much more. However, the interesting thing to me is that more or less every single one of them knows what they have done is wrong. Not only do they have a conscience, but nearly all of the teens I have worked with have been Christians. That means that they also know what God says about the things they have done. Thus, I have found that if I dig deep enough and ask enough questions, eventually the conscience explodes like a volcano and the feelings come pouring out:

> I feel so embarrassed!

> I feel so ashamed!

> I feel so dirty!

> I feel so *guilty*!

Those feelings of guilt can be very overwhelming, like you're carrying a massive weight on your shoulders. It can feel like you have to do everything in your power just to keep it all together somehow. But those guilty feelings need to be dealt with.

So how do you teens deal with guilt? In the same ways as other humans but with certain teen nuances. Here are some of the most common ways I see teens dealing with guilt. See if any ring a bell for you:

> Denial. Many are very well aware of what they have done. Many Christian teens know when they have sinned. But they don't want to come face to face with those sins or admit them. Maybe they're afraid to say something. Maybe they're afraid to show weakness. Maybe they don't want to let down dad or mom or

pastor or friends. Thus, they ignore the guilt. They bury it down deep in the emotional caverns of their hearts, hoping and praying that A) no one finds out or that B) they can somehow forget about it and not deal with it.

Excuses. Humans become expert excuse makers from little on. If you have siblings, you know. "But he hit me first . . . It was her idea to do that." You probably did it at recess in school, too. "He told me to . . . I wasn't the only one . . . But she was being mean." As we grow older, we become quite good at excuses, almost convincing ourselves that what we are saying is actually legit. "Mom, I don't listen to or say those words. I just like the music for the rhythm and the beats . . . I mean, everyone else is sleeping around . . . I wasn't the only one who was drinking. It was just one drink. Others drank more . . . She took the picture. That was her fault. If she didn't want me to send it to the whole school then she shouldn't have taken the pic or sent it to me . . . What does it matter if I cheated when it's just a little test for one dumb class? No one will care in five years."

Give up and give in. Related to the excuses category, many teens get stuck with this mentality. They feel like they've already been dirtied, so how can they be clean again? "Well it's too late. I've already smoked. I've already drank. Might as well do it again now." This is especially true with sexual sins. I've heard many teens say that once they crossed a certain line or lost their virginity they realized they could never get it back. In their minds, if they're already impure and can't get their purity back, they might as well carry on. Or related to this, many have tried fighting off temptations and sins, but they think it's just too hard. Not only do they give in to the sins, but they give up trying to stop.

Saying it's cool. I suppose this could also fit in the excuses category, but I think it deserves its own mention.

Peer pressure is a very real thing, and it can be extremely intense. I think that peer pressure has never been as intense as it is right now in the 21st century. In previous generations people would talk about things they did and pressure others into doing it, too. They would also see people on TV or in movies or magazines doing these things. But now, the pressure to do things is in your face 24/7 between all the media and social media outlets. With all of this influence, suddenly teens start to rationalize what they're doing. "Times have changed . . . This is what teens do these days . . . I don't want to be a loser. At least people like me and think I'm cool and popular when I do this. Everyone else is doing it."

Acting out. The last way I see teens dealing with guilt is a dangerous one. All of the previous ways are dangerous, but this way of handling guilt is particularly damaging to your faith. It goes hand-in-hand with giving up and giving in. But in this scenario, the guilt of sin becomes so overwhelming that the person overcompensates by acting out. They are trying to drown out their guilt somehow. Usually it's with something that gives them a certain high or good feeling, like sex or alcohol or pills or drugs, or simply general bad attitudes toward other people. Subconsciously, acting out is just another way to bury guilt further down. (Of course the thought never occurs to people that acting out with more sin will also heap on more guilt and make them feel worse!)

Any of these sound familiar? They sure do to me. Embarrassingly so. Too many times to count. But I think we need to have some real talk right now about guilt and ask ourselves some tough questions.

Question 1: Why do we do these things?

There's one big reason lurking down deep inside each of us—I want to be *justified*. I don't like feeling guilty. I don't like it when my conscience stings. I don't like it when I feel bad about myself. When I feel guilty and my conscience hurts, I know that means I'm also not quite right with God or with other people. I don't like that.

Thus, when I deny what I've done, or push blame onto others, or make excuses, or act like it's cool, or bury it by doing worse things—all of these are really just ways that I'm trying to justify myself. I'm doing anything and everything I can to make myself feel better because maybe, just maybe, I can convince myself that I'll be OK. Or in other words, I do these things because I'm trying desperately not to feel guilty.

Question 2: Have these things ever worked?

Let's be real here. You know the answer and so do I. No way, no how, not ever. NO! No matter how many excuses I make or how much I push things down or how cool I act—when the dust settles the same problem is still there—I have sinned and thus I am guilty.

Have you felt the burden of sin weighing down on you? Have you felt like a giant weight of guilt is crushing and suffocating you? Have you looked for ways to try and shake that guilty feeling, perhaps in some of the ways I mentioned?

When we are burdened by our sin we can feel overwhelmed, trapped, cornered, and condemned. It makes us want to blurt out through the tears —*I feel so guilty!*

When I feel like this, I need something different. I need some facts . . .

Fact: I Am Innocent

It would be hard for someone to feel more embarrassed or ashamed. He was caked in sweat and mud, so filthy that no one would want to come near him. But not only did he look dirty, he *felt* dirty. Far worse than smelling like manure or being covered in muck and mire were the stench and sight of his own sins. He felt *so* guilty.

He had dishonored his father and abandoned his family. He had lived the Hollywood life and squandered his entire inheritance. He slept with prostitutes. Now it was all gone, and he was so desperate that he was working (and eating!) with pigs—animals that were unclean in Jewish law.

He was at absolute rock bottom both physically and spiritually. There was nothing left to do except the most embarrassing thing he could think of—go back home and admit his guilt. He was so nervous that he even practiced and rehearsed what he was going to say: "Father, I have sinned against heaven and against you. I am no longer worthy to be called your son."[71]

But to his shock and surprise, even while he was still a distance from home, his father saw him, ran to him, embraced him, and kissed him. He welcomed him home with joy and dressed him in the finest robe and put a ring on his finger and held a feast to celebrate.

Jesus told this story of the prodigal son[72] to highlight several key points. If we go back to the beginning of Luke 15, we find out that there were plenty of self-righteous Jewish leaders who couldn't believe that Jesus was hanging out with "sinners," meaning the real "bad" people of society—at least in their eyes. Jesus used the bad attitude of the older brother who complained about the prodigal brother's welcome to point out the bad attitudes of these Jewish leaders. But Jesus also used the story to illustrate the depths of sin we quickly find ourselves in. The word *prodigal* is a word that means to be generous, lavish, or reckless to the point of being excessive and extravagant. The younger son was definitely *prodigal* in his sinful behavior. We often are, too.

---

[71] Luke 15:18–19
[72] Luke 15:11–32

But perhaps the most important point of this parable is that the word *prodigal* is better applied to someone else in the story—the father.[73] It was the father who was generous, lavish, excessive, and extravagant with his love. He didn't grill his son or ground him for the rest of his life. He didn't lock the door, shut the blinds, and pretend he wasn't home. He didn't say, "How could you do that to your family? You're dead to me!" No, instead he poured out extravagant love and forgiveness. In just this same way, our heavenly Father pours out his extravagant love on us. In the last chapter we looked at the facts that show us why we can be certain that we are loved by grace with a boundless *agape* love that never ends. Now we can look at what that love specifically means for us when we feel guilty like the prodigal son.

If there is one person who shows us his raw emotions and feelings of guilt more than anyone else in the Bible, it's most certainly King David. Talk about "keeping it 100"! You can't find anything more real and raw than David baring his soul in several of his psalms. Aside from honestly sharing his emotions and feelings, it also becomes very real to us because we know why David wrote these things—Bathsheba.

Remember that story? David was out on his balcony one night and saw this hottie bathing on her balcony. Lust led to coveting,[74] which led to a plot, which led to adultery, which led to another plot, which led to the murder of Bathsheba's husband, which led to a pile of lies, which led to a TON of guilt. Eventually, when David was exposed by the prophet Nathan, all his guilt erupted like Old Faithful.

In the heading to Psalm 51, we are told that David wrote this psalm after Nathan had visited him. Read the psalm. Go ahead

---

[73] Timothy Keller wrote an excellent little book about this called *The Prodigal God*. Check it out!

[74] To covet means to have a strong desire for something, especially something that doesn't belong to you—such as someone else's wife.

and take a break from this book for a few minutes and then come back after this paragraph. Read all of Psalm 51 and see if you can feel David's hurt and pain as he begs, "Have mercy on me, O God . . . Create in me a pure heart . . . Do not cast me from your presence . . . Deliver me."[75] His guilty conscience bursts off the page.

David is even more clear and specific about how he felt in Psalm 32. Listen to David express his feelings of guilt there:

> When I kept silent,
> my bones wasted away
> through my groaning all day long.
> For day and night
> your hand was heavy on me;
> my strength was sapped
> as in the heat of summer.[76]

These are the feelings we discussed a little bit ago. This is what guilt can do to you. It can crush you like a massive weight. It can make you feel sick and worn out as you waste away spiritually on the inside. It's the epitome of when someone might say they are "dying on the inside."

But the beauty of David's psalms lies in the resolution that he brings to us. While David felt so horrible, he also knew the answer to his guilt and shares it with us:

> Then I acknowledged my sin to you
> and did not cover up my iniquity.
> I said, "I will confess
> my transgressions to the LORD."
> And you forgave
> the guilt of my sin.[77]

---

[75] Psalm 51:1, 10–11, 14
[76] Psalm 32:3–4
[77] Psalm 32:5

This is the amazing grace of God's love we talked about last chapter. This is the lavish, *prodigal* love of the father in Jesus' parable we just reviewed. His love moves him to have mercy on us and forgive us.

That word *forgive* is a really important word. Christians talk about forgiveness a lot. Even non-Christians talk about forgiveness. It's important to understand what the word actually means though. To *forgive* means *to send or throw away*. I like to think of it like you're crumpling up paper garbage and throwing it away in a garbage can and then that trash is taken away forever to the dump. Or think of it like something you put in a package and send far away, never to return again. That's what God has done with your sins. He has sent them away. He has forgiven them.

However, understand that God has not just taken up your sin and tossed them in the trash five feet from you or taken them to the city dump. He hasn't just packaged up your sins and sent them to the other side of the world. No, that's not even close to far enough! Listen again to the incredible words we looked at in the last chapter. Surprise, surprise! David wrote these words too:

> The LORD is compassionate and gracious,
>   slow to anger, abounding in love . . .
> as far as the east is from the west,
>   so far has he removed our transgressions from us.[78]

It is not even possible to measure how far God has removed and sent away (forgiven) your sins from you. Wherever it is that the east ends in our universe, and wherever it is that the west ends (Good luck figuring that out!), and however far apart those two endpoints are—that's how far away your sins have been removed from you.

The prophet Micah pictures forgiveness in a different but equally beautiful way. Here's what he says:

---

[78] Psalm 103:8, 12

> Who is a God like you,
>> who pardons sin and forgives the transgression
>> of the remnant of his inheritance?
> You do not stay angry forever
>> but delight to show mercy.
> You will again have compassion on us;
>> you will tread our sins underfoot
>> and hurl all our iniquities into the depths of the sea.[79]

Have you learned about the Mariana Trench in science or geography classes yet? Near this area of the Pacific Ocean, the depth of the water is over 35,000 feet deep. That's more than six miles! No human could possibly survive down there. But that's where God has buried your sin, so to speak. It's drowned and never coming back—a picture all the more meaningful when you think about the washing and waters of baptism!

This forgiveness is yours in Jesus. Early on in his ministry, it was John the Baptist who pointed at him and said, "Look, the Lamb of God, who takes away the sin of the world!"[80] How right he was! Jesus is the Lamb who took away / sent away / removed / forgave your sins by drowning them not in ocean water but in the flood of his own blood.

What is gnawing at your conscience? What keeps you awake at night? What are you hiding from your parents, your pastor, your friends? What sin(s) are you trying desperately to forget because you feel so guilty? Dear teen, know this:

> **Fact #1** – You are *innocent* because you are forgiven. You may feel so guilty about something you have done. Maybe you simply feel guilty about the sum total of all that you have ever done. But know this: Your guilt is gone! God has removed and sent away your sins forever for the sake of Jesus Christ! You have been washed clean

---

[79] Micah 7:18–19
[80] John 1:29

in his blood and in the waters of baptism! You are
innocent in his sight!

Another feeling that accompanies the feeling of guilt—you
could say it's a subcategory of guilt—is the feeling of being dirty.
I find that this is especially true when people sin with or against
their own body. Certainly there are many who feel dirty in
general because of the sins they have committed. But this feeling
is super-sensitive when it comes to your body. When teens drink
alcohol or smoke or take substances that are illegal, there is a
very real feeling of hurting, harming, or dirtying your own body.
Yet in my experience, this is even more so the case when it
comes to sexual sins. God talks often in the Bible about having
pure thoughts, words, and actions, especially when it comes to
the gift of sex he gave for husband and wife to enjoy. When
teens don't follow God's guidelines for sex or purity, very
quickly they find themselves feeling dirty, as though they are
permanently stained and spotted from their sins. Listen to how
David talks about this in that famous Psalm 51:

> Have mercy on me, O God . . .
>   blot out my transgressions.
> Wash away all my iniquity
>   and cleanse me from my sin.
> Cleanse me with hyssop, and I will be clean;
>   wash me, and I will be whiter than snow.[81]

David was pleading with God for a cleansing from all his sins,
and in his incredible mercy, God listened to the cries and
confession of a dirty sinner. In the same way, God mercifully
hears and answers us now, too. It was about 300 years after
David that God made this mercy very clear using very beautiful
imagery. After 16 straight verses leveling the people of Israel
with their sins through the prophet Isaiah, God changes
directions and says this:

---

[81] Psalm 51:1–2, 7

"Come now, let us settle the matter,"
    says the LORD.
"Though your sins are like scarlet,
    they shall be as white as snow;
though they are red as crimson,
    they shall be like wool."[82]

Even though they were as stained and filthy as your parents' white carpet that you spilled your grape juice on, God was going to treat them like they were crystal clear and clean. What kind of soap or detergent or bleach could possibly do this? The answer is again, Jesus! "The blood of Jesus, his Son, purifies us from all sin."[83]

The apostle Paul also used beautiful language to describe how we have been cleansed through Christ. In Ephesians Paul describes Jesus as the heavenly Groom and us as the bride that has been dirtied and stained with sin. But look at what our heavenly Groom has done for us:

> Christ loved the church and gave himself up for her to make her holy, cleansing her by the washing with water through the word, and to present her to himself as a radiant church, without stain or wrinkle or any other blemish, but holy and blameless.[84]

No person would love or marry a bride as "ugly" as we are. We are dirty, stained, and blemished—guilty—from all our sins against our Groom. But Jesus gave himself up for us. He cleansed us and washed us, both with his blood and the waters of baptism. Then he presented us as his radiant, beautiful, and blameless bride.

---

[82] Isaiah 1:18
[83] 1 John 1:7
[84] Ephesians 5:25–27

Have you done something that you are ashamed of? Is there something that haunts you, that you can't seem to get rid of like a dirty stain on clean clothing? Does your sin make you feel dirty? Then know this next fact:

> **Fact #2** – You are innocent because you are forgiven and *washed clean in the blood of Christ.* No matter how dirty you may feel, the fact is that the most potent cleaner ever—the divine bleach of Jesus' blood—has made you clean and beautiful in God's sight!

This then brings us back to the courtroom scene, something we explored in Chapter 3. If you were on trial and someone wanted to accuse you but there was absolutely no record of any crime being committed and absolutely no evidence at all, then it would be a pretty easy court case. It would be a slam dunk decision. The verdict would come quickly. You would be declared not guilty on the spot.

That is exactly the case with you. You are forgiven! Your sin is so far removed from you that there is no record of any crime in God's book. You have been washed clean by the blood of Jesus and now stand spotless in God's courtroom. You are not guilty in God's sight. Or using the Bible's language again, you have been *justified.*

The apostle Paul writes a lot about this not guilty verdict in the Bible. Here are two very clear and very beautiful examples:

> You were washed, you were sanctified, you were justified in the name of the Lord Jesus Christ and by the Spirit of our God.[85]

> All are justified freely by his grace through the redemption that came by Christ Jesus.[86]

---

[85] 1 Corinthians 6:11
[86] Romans 3:24

Jesus is the one who has brought you this not guilty verdict. But unlike paying for your prom dress or tux to be dry cleaned, and unlike having to pay bail to get out of jail, this cleansing and not guilty verdict come to you freely without cost. That verdict is yours to keep now *and* forever. Check out these words from Revelation that show us that this verdict is ours to keep eternally:

> Whoever has ears, let them hear what the Spirit says to the churches. To the one who is victorious, I will give some of the hidden manna. I will also give that person a white stone with a new name written on it, known only to the one who receives it.[87]

In John's time, it was common for juries to announce their verdict of "not guilty" at a court case with a white stone. This picture language is a beautiful way to communicate to us that our court victory is finalized and will last forever.

What a blessing! What a blessing to be forgiven, to have all our sins removed, and to stand with a new and innocent life before God! David captured this as he began Psalm 32:

> Blessed is the one
> > whose transgressions are forgiven,
> > whose sins are covered.
> Blessed is the one
> > whose sin the LORD does not count against them
> > and in whose spirit is no deceit.[88]

How blessed we are to have this new identity of "innocent" in God's sight through Jesus! That brings us to a third fact.

Fact #3 – You are innocent. You are forgiven and washed clean in the blood of Christ, and therefore, *you*

---

[87] Revelation 2:17
[88] Psalm 32:1–2

are justified in God's sight now and forever. The verdict is in and it stands in your favor for all eternity.

Summary

One thing I have noticed about teens today that is different from generations past is this: teens find themselves *deep* in sin *very* quickly. It takes nothing more than a few taps on a phone to be immersed in sin on the Internet, or in inappropriate conversations or pictures sent back and forth, or in coordinating plans for parties.

How quickly we all can find ourselves deep into sin though! Like David stuck in a web of wickedness and lies with the whole Bathsheba debacle, we often find ourselves tangled and ensnared in sin so fast. All these sins we commit prick our consciences and sting. They make us feel ashamed, embarrassed, and dirty. Most of all, they make us feel guilty. But even though you may feel guilty—and let's be honest, even though we *are* guilty—we can focus on the facts. Let's review them:

> Fact #1 – You are forgiven. God has sent your sin away.

> Fact #2 – You are washed clean in the blood of Jesus.

> Fact #3 – You are justified and declared not guilty now and forever.

All of those facts are yours in Jesus. No matter what you have done—no matter how big or small, overt or covert, accidental or purposeful—no matter what sin, you are innocent in God's sight. This is part of your new identity in Christ. As Jesus was perfect, innocent, and righteous, so too are you now. Amazing!

Oh, and good news! Your pure and perfect wedding clothes aren't rentals. This new identity of innocence in Christ is yours to keep. Forever! Later in Revelation, John records a vision he had of a multitude no one could count in heaven wearing white robes. The question arose, "These in white robes—who are they, and where did they come from?"[89] Here was the answer:

> These are they who have come out of the great
> tribulation; they have washed their robes and made them
> white in the blood of the Lamb.[90]

Jesus has washed you clean. You have a righteous robe that was purchased at the cross and guaranteed at the tomb. But it's a garment that you'll wear for all eternity as you stand innocent in God's sight forever and ever.

Dear teen, trust the facts. Trust God's words.

You *are* innocent!

---

[89] Revelation 7:13
[90] Revelation 7:14

Chapter 7

Feeling: I Feel Worthless

vs.

Fact: I Am Priceless

Danny wanted to throw his phone across the room. His alarm clock kept buzzing in his ear, but he was so tired that he kept hitting snooze instead of turning it off. With blurred vision he was staring at the ceiling through the sleep-crusties in his eyes. Another day? Already? It's only Wednesday! "I literally can't," he thought. "I can't do today. I can't get out of bed."

This sort of snuck up on Danny over the last couple months. Gradually over time it was harder and harder to get up, get out of bed, and get to school. Thoughts like, "What does it matter? Who even cares? No one would miss me!" continually crossed his mind.

After all, Danny was a C student on his best days—and that was even when he gave some effort and tried. He sat in the back or the corner for most of his classes. His teachers rarely called on him, if they even looked in his direction. He didn't really do anything after school since after freshman year he got cut from basketball and he quit football because he felt like the coach didn't like him (though if he was honest, he would admit he really didn't want to put in the effort or time). Danny tried some other after school groups but quickly realized that they were weird. But to be honest again, Danny knew that he was the one who was into some very unusual hobbies and didn't fit in.

Danny's friend game was also pretty lame. He would watch all the cool kids walk through the hallways like they were hot stuff and it drove him crazy. Did any of them even know he existed? He was sure that all the pretty girls rolled their eyes when they looked at him. Most of the time Danny felt like he was alone because one of his best friends had moved across the country and the other two he was close with worked all the time.

Oh yeah, then there was work. Danny had a job because his dad made him get one. That was a disaster. He got a job doing something he thought could be fairly mindless and easy (and that didn't involve talking to people). But apparently he was a pretty terrible stock boy at the grocery store because the manager was all over his case all day long about how he didn't break down boxes right or how he needed to tuck in his shirt or just in general about why "his generation was so lazy." Blah, blah, blah.

At least work was a reason to get out of the house. Home was maybe the worst because home is where his reality smacked him in the face. Danny was the youngest of three siblings. His older brother was a stud muffin of a football player and super popular. He currently was playing D-2 football and living his best college life. His sister, the oldest, was academic top ten in her class and got a boat load of college scholarships. She was about to graduate and enter law school.

You see the problem was that Danny felt all this was rubbed in his face constantly by his parents. "When are you going to start working hard like your brother? . . . How come you don't try like your sister? . . . Did you pick your college yet? . . . What are you going to do with yourself? . . . Danny, when are you going to get your act together?"

The only place Danny felt some sort of refuge was locked in his room listening to music and binging random shows or movies. Work was horrible. His family was just too much. School was stupid. Social media was even more stupid to him. In his bad moments, Danny wondered who would even notice or care if he was gone. In his worst moments, Danny had thoughts run through his mind about how to make that happen. But more than anything, there was this overwhelmingly dull pain that he couldn't seem to overcome. The pain was from this thought—*I feel so worthless.*

Feeling Worthless

Everyone likes to feel valued. This is a natural thing to every human. It's instinctual. It's part of who we are. There is no one who naturally says, "You know what? I want to be a completely valueless and meaningless person with no reason for existence. That would be really nice. Hope I can achieve that some day!" Anyone who talked like that would be the mayor of Crazy Town.

Instead, we all want to feel like we have worth and value. Think back to when you were a little kid. Dad is doing a house project or mom is baking a cake. What do kids ask? "Can I help? Can I do it? What can I do?" Then when the task is done the child exclaims, "Look what I did!" Certainly there is pride in accomplishment, but the child is also glad that they contributed, they did something, and they had *value.*

This continues as you get older. It's an awesome feeling when the captains pick you first for the kickball team. They need you! It's a terrible feeling to get picked last for the kickball team. I guess no one needed you! It's a great feeling to get some playing time; it's an awful feeling to watch from the bench. It's amazing to have a lead role in the school play, but a painful feeling to be part of the chorus for yet another year. In school you want to feel like you have worth or value.

The same is true socially. If you have friends that help you and support you and encourage you, if you have friends that always got your back and are your ride or dies, it feels wonderful to have a group of people that you value and that value you. But if you feel like people look at you funny, or talk behind your back, or stab you in the back, or ignore you, then you start to feel worthless and like you have no value.

This is only amplified with social media because everything happens in real time and right in front of your face. You can see everyone's business all at the same time and compare it to what seems to be your lame, loser life. If your meme goes viral, if people talk about your funny video, if you get lots of clicks—these make you feel good about yourself. It makes you feel like people care, like you have some worth or value.

But the opposite can happen in the blink of an eye on social media, too. You realize that almost nobody likes your pics, even the people you tag in them and even when you beg, "like my recent." You constantly see pictures of groups of friends chilling, but you're not in any of those pics. Everyone else gets the praise, the attention, the clicks, the likes, but you get nothing and always seem to be missing out. Doesn't anyone value you?

You'll find the desire to feel value or worth only continues as you get older, and in some ways becomes more intense. Think about some extreme examples of professional athletes. Name the superstar and you will find that when their contract comes to an end, they will be holding out for the biggest offer from the best teams. Then they are insulted when someone offers them less money, especially less than another player. Why? They want to feel like valued! After all, they do compete for the Most *Valuable* Player award!

In the same way, as you get older you'll find similar thoughts crossing your mind with your career. Do I really bring value to this company? Maybe I should use my skills somewhere else? Does this business really value me? Do they pay me what I'm worth? Many a midlife crisis has started as people contemplate their worth or value in life.

Finally, I want to come back to the home. There is no place where there is greater importance for feeling value and worth than at home. I have worked with countless teens who have lots of great things going for them in life with school, athletics, or friends, but they are a mess if things aren't right with dad or mom. It's not just my observations though. There is endless research that tells us how important it is for parents to praise their children, communicate their love, and thus show that their children have value. Sadly, there are many ways that we parents fail our children and do just the opposite. Here are some examples:

> Parents aren't around. Maybe one parent isn't in the picture. Maybe there was a divorce and one parent doesn't contribute much. Maybe the parents are just too busy with their own stuff (usually work is the excuse). Or maybe the parents are just emotionally distant and kind of lazy as they are not present for their children emotionally. But when parents aren't there for you—at home, at events or games, for difficult times—you start to feel like you have no value.

> Parents are too demanding. In this situation, parents put their kids in every activity, every sport, or every program imaginable. They spread their children way too thin, but then expect them to be great at everything. They demand great grades and perfect effort. They expect big college scholarships. They won't settle for any type of career path except what they think is best and most ideal. When you don't think you meet parental expectations, you feel like you have no value.

> Parents are too controlling. Similar to the last one, the parents act like they know best about everything. Since that is the case, they control your every last move and

motion. They track you with GPS. They enforce earlier curfews than anyone else and let you go out less than anyone else. But when you feel suffocated, like you aren't trusted, or like you have no freedoms, you quickly feel like you have no value.

Parents aren't understanding. This one can be kind of subtle, yet very impactful. Usually this plays out with parents saying stuff like, "It was no big deal back in my day. I got through it. How come you can't?" Or, "Seriously! Why are you like this? Get over it!" Or even, "It's not going to kill you. It'll be alright. Just move on." They probably mean well. Parents want their kids to be tough and often try to communicate that everyone has tough times and that if they made it through, so can their kids. Yet when you feel like you aren't understood, or that no one cares to take the time to understand, then again you feel like you have no value.

Have you experienced any of these before? A lot? A little? One of them? All of them? If you have, I have two things to say to you. 1) I'm very sorry. I'm sorry to hear that you may have hurt and that things aren't always great for you at home. But, 2) Cut your parents a little slack. Yes, there are some who are just failing miserably. If that's your experience, then I really hurt for you. But in general, I see that parents are trying. There is no parenting manual, and they are sinners, too. So they are going to make mistakes—a lot of them. Keep trying to communicate with them! Maybe you could seek the help of someone else like a counselor or a pastor to work with your family?

I encourage you to work on these things with your parents because it is so important for you to feel worth and value at home. That is the foundational place that God has given to you for love, support, and encouragement. In other words, it's the first and foremost place that you should feel valued. So when you don't, there is a lot of hurt and pain that come along the way.

When there is hurt and pain, though, we have to deal with it. That leads to another world of issues. The proper way to handle hurt is to work on it through communication, love, forgiveness, and effort. The sad thing is that more often than not, when teens feel no worth or value, they deal with it by changing their behavior. Here are some common examples:

Overcompensation. This one is tricky and many probably don't even know they are doing it. It usually goes something like this: You don't feel like you fit in. Maybe it's your weight or how you think you look or you're not as good at sports as your peers or you don't seem to be as popular. Over time you gradually start to overcompensate with your behavior. You become the class clown. You are over-the-top goofy or silly. You are loud and obnoxious. But what you are doing without knowing it is trying to get attention. If people laugh at you because you're funny and the center of attention, then you must have some value!

Acting out. This is another way that teens often try to catch the attention of parents or teachers or their peers. You are disrespectful in the classroom. You are defiant and rude and sarcastic with your parents, always fighting and arguing like you're a top-notch defense attorney pleading your case. Maybe if you're over the top they will get your point? Maybe if you call them out and put them on shout they'll actually listen or care? Maybe some of these overcompensating behaviors will get someone to notice and value you?

Destructive behavior. Sadly, it follows very easily that if you don't feel any worth or value from others, you won't treat yourself with any worth or value. So instead of pursuing what is God-pleasing or best for yourself or your body, you start pursuing other things. What makes you look cool or tough or popular or sexy? What makes you feel good? What takes the hurt away? There are many teens who try to cope with their pain or try to find self-worth with alcohol, drugs, pills, sex, or any number of other things. The reason I call this destructive behavior is that, tragically, it usually makes teens feel worse! In the end you will see what you have done and feel even less worth or value about yourself.

Self-harm. I wish I could say this is a rare way for teens to handle feelings of lacking worth or value, but regrettably it is very common. When some feel no worth or value they often start to wonder whether they even matter. Does anyone care? What if I'm not around? Would anyone care if I'm not around? Sometimes those thoughts lead to actions. Purposeful binge drinking, pushing limits on pills, over-vaping, cutting, and worse things are harmful next steps when teens are wrestling with low self-esteem and self-worth. "If no one else values me, why should I value myself?" some might think.[91]

Have you felt before like you have no value? Have you felt this at home, at school, with friends, or online? All of the above? Have you found yourself acting out in any of these previous ways? A little? A lot? Thought about harming yourself? Done it?

These are painful experiences that leave us feeling like we have no value. They leave us thinking—*I feel worthless.*

When I feel like this, I need something different. I need some facts . . .

---

[91] These kinds of behaviors and thoughts are *always* serious. ALWAYS. If you see or hear a friend who has these things going on, *always* help them. Self-harm and suicide talk or actions should *always* be taken seriously and *never* be joked about. It's not funny. If you want to be a real friend, get the help of an adult. ALWAYS. If you personally are wrestling with those things, *always* seek help. It may be embarrassing or difficult, but it is so important! And if you can't find anyone that you think will help, then contact me! I would be glad to help. My Email is phil.huebner17@gmail.com.

Fact: I Am Priceless

How many things must have been going through their minds? Probably the same kinds of things people usually drift off during sermons to think about: Why doesn't my family respect me? It's like they don't even care! How come no one notices me? Why do unbelievers have to make my life so difficult? Why is everything in my life difficult? Does anyone care? Does God even care?

But as Jesus sat down on a hillside one day amid crowds of people, he caught their attention right from the beginning with the opening to his famous Sermon on the Mount. "Blessed are the poor in spirit . . . Blessed are those who mourn . . . Blessed are the meek . . . Blessed are those who are persecuted."[92] Many must have thought, "Thank you, Jesus! Thank you for saying I am blessed! But wait a second! I still have so much going on in my life! How do I know I have any worth or value to God?"

Jesus went on with his sermon to shake their cores a bit, teaching them with very serious words about godly living and God-pleasing prayers. Then he addressed the elephant in the room (or on the hill, I guess)—worry. So many problems in life! So many worries! It's a common problem to all humans, even Christians, stemming from the thought deep inside that God doesn't care and God won't help. "Am I not worth anything to God?" Jesus knew their hearts and had beautiful words for them and for us to ponder. Listen to his compassionate words:

> Therefore I tell you, do not worry about your life, what you will eat or drink; or about your body, what you will wear. Is not life more than food, and the body more than clothes? Look at the birds of the air; they do not sow or reap or store away in barns, and yet your heavenly Father feeds them. Are you not much more valuable than they? Can any one of you by worrying add a single hour to your life?

---

[92] Matthew 5:3–10

> And why do you worry about clothes? See how the
> flowers of the field grow. They do not labor or spin. Yet
> I tell you that not even Solomon in all his splendor was
> dressed like one of these. If that is how God clothes the
> grass of the field, which is here today and tomorrow is
> thrown into the fire, will he not much more clothe
> you—you of little faith?[93]

This seems to be an illustration that hit home with the people.
He used a similar one on a different occasion:

> Are not two sparrows sold for a penny? Yet not one of
> them will fall to the ground outside your Father's care.
> And even the very hairs of your head are all numbered.
> So don't be afraid; you are worth more than many
> sparrows.[94]

Jesus' point is very profound. Our God is so great and so
knowledgeable and so caring that he knows, feeds, and cares
about every little bird. He even carefully clothes every flimsy
flower or blade of grass, things that are plucked or cut or blown
away in an instant. So if God cares that much about little birds
or flowers or grass, how much more doesn't God care for you?
If even birds or flowers or grass have value to God, how much
more don't *we* have value to God!

Jesus went on to teach that everywhere he went. But it wasn't
only his sermons that taught the worth of people. His actions
spoke louder than words. Jesus didn't just hang with the cool
kids of Jewish society—the rich, the powerful, the Pharisees, the
priests. Jesus loved and cared for everyone, even the social
outcasts like the tax collectors, the prostitutes, the lepers, the
poor, and the needy.

---

93 Matthew 6:25–30
94 Matthew 10:29–31

Yet no sermon of Jesus' words or actions had more volume or a bigger exclamation point than the one he preached on the cross. There Jesus gave his life—a divine, perfect, holy, and righteous life—for the entire world. His life and death for all shows that God values everyone in the world. It's been that way since the beginning. So let's go back to the beginning right now and explore how much value God has placed on you!

Is it even possible to fathom the nothingness that existed before creation? What was it like for there to be nothing but God— Father, Son, and Holy Spirit? And how could it be that he just "was" forever and ever, eternally before us? These are questions no one can answer perfectly. I'm not afraid to say that. Put them on your question list for when you get to heaven. It's going to be a long list!

There in that unfathomable nothingness God could have just chilled forever. He is perfect. All of the nothingness was perfect (however that's even possible!?). He wasn't lonely or bored or itching for a project to take on. Yet in his wisdom and love he decided to start creating. So he spoke. "Let there be light!"[95] and it happened. There was light. Just like that. Out of nowhere. In a vast nothingness of darkness that didn't know what non-darkness was, there was suddenly light.

Step by step and day by day God continued to create, which literally means to make out of nothing (and thus something only God can do). Sky. Land and seas and vegetation. Sun, moon, and stars. Fish and birds. Animals. Each day more miracles. Each day the complexity vastly increasing. Go ahead and pick any of those days and you could spend a hundred lifetimes studying the sky or water and all its molecules, or the planets and stars, or living creatures and you still wouldn't gather all the information there is to know about each. But God knows it all because God planned it all, created it all, and pieced it together perfectly like the most ridiculous bajillion-piece puzzle.

---

[95] Genesis 1:3

111

On any day he could have stopped because it was unfathomably amazing. As God noted each day, "It was good." Umm. Yes. Understatement of eternity, Lord! It was *great!* It was *perfect!*

It was good, but it wasn't complete. Not yet. God had something else in mind, something to be the exclamation point at the end, the cherry on top, the crown jewel of a precious creation. Humans.

Think about all the steps God took to point to human life as being precious and special:

1) He created humans last.

2) He created humans in his image. Now that is not to say that Adam and Eve were twins with God like Mary Kate and Ashley Olson.[96] Rather, this means that Adam and Eve had the likeness of God in their characteristics. They weren't little gods. They were holy and righteous *like* God. Their will was perfectly aligned with God's will.

3) He created humans to have rule and dominion over all things. In other words, this awesomely amazing universe was created just for us to rule over and enjoy!

4) He breathed into Adam "the breath of life."[97] Interestingly, the word for breath in Hebrew is *nephesh.* Not only does it mean breath, but it could also be translated as *spirit.* This would likely be when God gave to human beings a soul, a conscience, a rational mind, and everything that sets us apart spiritually as being much different and much more valuable than plants or animals.

---

[96] I sure hope teens still know who they are when they read this. Otherwise younger me would grieve!

[97] Genesis 2:7

5) He created Eve in a special and memorable way and gave her to Adam to have a special relationship. This was not just any mating partnership, but a special relationship called "marriage" where a man and a woman come together as one flesh and form a family.

The glory, honor, value, and worth given to human beings is beyond expression. Perhaps we can only join King David to praise God this way:

> LORD, our Lord,
> how majestic is your name in all the earth!
> You have set your glory
> in the heavens.
> When I consider your heavens,
> the work of your fingers,
> the moon and the stars,
> which you have set in place,
> what is mankind that you are mindful of them,
> human beings that you care for them?
> You have made them a little lower than the angels
> and crowned them with glory and honor.
> You made them rulers over the works of your hands;
> you put everything under their feet:
> all flocks and herds,
> and the animals of the wild,
> the birds in the sky,
> and the fish in the sea,
> all that swim the paths of the seas.
> LORD, our Lord,
> how majestic is your name in all the earth![98]

---

[98] Psalm 8:1, 3–9. Important next-level Bible knowledge note: This psalm is super cool because it also points to Christ. The word *mankind* can also be translated *son of man*, which is a phrase that often points to Jesus. Hebrews 2:5–9 also quotes this psalm in reference to Jesus. Thus, it would seem this psalm points to the value of *both* Christ *and* humans—an all the more awesome thought when considering our identity and value in Jesus!

This is why things like violence, murder, wars, euthanasia, abortion, genocide, racism, and other sins are such evil tragedies. Each one devalues human life by hating, hurting, harming, or ending human life. God created human life and clearly set it apart as sacred and special—to be valued more than anything else in the universe.

Have you struggled with feelings of low self-worth? Has it been hard to find the approval of others, even those who are supposed to value you the most like your parents? If you have had feelings of being worthless, understand this first fact:

> **Fact #1** – You are *priceless* because you have human life. God gave you life as he has every other creature. You wouldn't be here if God didn't want you to be. But you are. You have life and that life is valuable because God set it apart to be sacred and special above any other creature.

There are some though who have what we would call a "deist" view of God. Basically this means that God is like a grand clockmaker in the sky who wound up the universe and now just lets things run on their own. The view is that God is distant and far off and out of touch. Some even try to mesh this with evolutionism saying that God got everything started in the beginning, but it has been random chance and evolution since then.

People with these kinds of false ideas still feel worthless quite often because to them God is not a very close or personal God. Sometimes these ideas rub off on us, too. "What does God really care, anyways? What does God even know about me? I'm just one little speck in an endless universe!"

Nothing could be farther from the truth. Not only did God give you human life, which is special and precious and valuable, but

he also had personal involvement in making you who you are.
Listen to these precious words of King David:[99]

> You have searched me, LORD,
>   and you know me.
> For you created my inmost being;
>   you knit me together in my mother's womb.
> I praise you because I am fearfully and wonderfully
>   made;
>   your works are wonderful,
>   I know that full well.
> My frame was not hidden from you
>   when I was made in the secret place,
>   when I was woven together in the depths of the
>   earth.
> Your eyes saw my unformed body;
>   all the days ordained for me were written in your
>   book
>   before one of them came to be.[100]

Have you watched someone do needlework before? Maybe
knitting or crocheting? The work is very careful and precise. If
the person working has any kind of skill, it's not random either.
There is a plan in mind to make a beautiful pattern or design.

How much more so is this true with you! God knit you together
in your mother's womb. Even when you were first conceived
and no one even knew you existed, God did. He made and wove
you together "in the secret place" in the womb. God carefully
crafted you to be you!

That's worth reflecting on for just a moment in today's world.
Today you can scroll through pictures in seconds of all the "hot"

---

[99] Someday, God-willing, you will be gifted the blessing of a child. And on
that day, I pray you find your way to this psalm, Psalm 139. I know of no
parent who could possibly hold their precious newborn and read these words
without tears in their eyes!
[100] Psalm 139:1, 13–16

and "sexy" people of the world. Billions of dollars and endless hours are spent by people trying to attain a certain image, trying to improve themselves, trying to look better. From silly things like photo scrubbing, touchups, and filters, to cosmetics and makeup, to major things like plastic surgeries including breast implants, nose jobs, lip injections, and more—the world is constantly saying, "You made a mistake, God! I'm not good enough!"

But listen to David and ponder his words carefully: "I praise you because I am fearfully and wonderfully made."[101] God did not make a mistake with you. How you look, your personality, your characteristics, your biological sex, your skin color—all of that was just as God the Master-Potter formed you, the clay.

There is one more profound verse we need to rewind on and ponder some more in that beautiful psalm. Verse 16: "Your eyes saw my unformed body; all the days ordained for me were written in your book before one of them came to be." Let that sink in. Even before you existed—other parts of the Bible would tell us even before the creation of the world—God knew you. He knew who you would be, what you would be like, when you would live, and how long you would live. I don't think I even have words to describe how special that is, so I'm just going to jump right into pointing out our next important fact:

> **Fact #2** – You are priceless because you have human life and because *God specifically, carefully, and meticulously made you to be you.* He made you. He formed you. He knew you before you even existed. With such incredible care and attention from our almighty God it is so clear— you have value!

I suppose there might be some of you who are very spiritually wise and still have a problem with your worth and value. Maybe the thought process goes something like this, "This is so

---

[101] Psalm 139:14

incredible that God has given me life and has made me specially and uniquely, but oh boy have I messed up! I have sinned *so much*! How could I do that to God and how could he ever love me? I am worthless to him!"

That seems to be what Adam and Eve were thinking. Here they were shortly after creation[102] in this perfect paradise that they had full rule over, and they broke the one command God gave them. It's not even a meme. They literally had one job to do— not eat from that one tree. But they did. OK, so they did a lot more than that. They questioned God. They doubted his good gifts to him. They coveted the fruit. They were greedy for more knowledge and power. They didn't help each other as husband and wife to run away from temptation. *And* they ate the fruit. Yup. Big time mess up. Big time sin—and they knew it.

Do you remember what happened next? They *immediately* realized that their relationships were ruined—both with each other and with their God. First, they sewed together fig leaves and covered themselves up because they were naked. I always find that fascinating. There was no one else on the face of the earth except those two—husband and wife—and they felt the need to cover themselves up. Sin brings instant shame and embarrassment!

Yet this is even more so true with God. So the next thing they did was hide. If they were embarrassed and ashamed of their bodies in front of each other, just imagine how terrified they were as they tried to hide from their God! Think back to when you were little and you did something wrong and the thought crossed your mind, "Oh no! Dad/Mom is going to kill me!" Well in this instance that would be a legit concern. Here was this perfect universe, a perfect paradise that God had made and

---

[102] Don't you wonder how long they made it after creation before they sinned? The story of creation ends with Genesis 2 and the Fall happens in Genesis 3. Did they even make it 10 hours? A day? A week?? Longer? Add it to your list of questions for heaven.

handed them the keys to, and they completely blew it. Like really, really blew it. And they knew it. God would have had every right to squash them like ants, to blow them into oblivion and just start over again. But he didn't!

Sure, there would be consequences. God told them how their lives would be much harder now, both as individual males and females and in their relationships with each other. And yes, there was now going to be physical death.[103] But before any of those consequences were ever spoken, God had a proclamation of good news:[104]

> And I will put enmity
>   between you and the woman,
>   and between your offspring and hers;
> he will crush your head,
>   and you will strike his heel.[105]

God is speaking to the devil here. God was going to put enmity (hatred, strife, discord) not only between Satan and Eve but also between his offspring (unbelievers) and hers (believers). But then, God announced something incredible—HE. A third party. A "he" was going to enter the picture. Satan would get a little strike on his heel, but "he" was going to ultimately crush Satan's head. You probably could guess if you didn't know. That "he" is Jesus.

Ponder that astounding mercy for a moment. Instead of wiping disobedient sinners off the face of the earth and starting over, God made a promise of love and forgiveness that he would save them through a promised One to come. Others with many more Bible-ninja mad skills than I have said that the entire Bible is really nothing more than a commentary on that one verse and

---

[103] Genesis 3:16–19

[104] By the way, did you know the word *gospel* literally means *good news*? The following is the first gospel promise of the Bible!

[105] Genesis 3:15

promise of God. I like that and totally agree. The whole rest of the Bible is the story of how God made good on that one promise through Jesus Christ, the promised Savior.

It is in Jesus Christ then that we see just how much God values human life, even though humans are sinful and disobedient. God values human life so much that he would give his own life to save it. Check out these verses:

> In him we have redemption through his blood, the forgiveness of sins, in accordance with the riches of God's grace that he lavished on us.[106]

God poured out the riches of his grace on us sinners to forgive us, and thus we have *redemption*. Redemption is another fancy-pants Bible word. Technically, to *redeem* means to *buy back*. It was a term that was often used in their Greek and Roman times when someone, like a slave or servant, had their freedom bought back when the ransom price was paid.

The ransom price to redeem you, to buy you back from death and hell, was infinitely more than Bill Gates and Jeff Bezos combined could ever pay for. It's a price no human could pay. So God did. Listen to Peter explain it:

> For you know that it was not with perishable things such as silver or gold that you were redeemed . . . but with the precious blood of Christ, a lamb without blemish or defect. He was chosen before the creation of the world, but was revealed in these last times for your sake.[107]

Only God himself could pay a price so steep. Only God himself could have a perfect and holy life to take your place. Only God himself could have a death so powerful that it could take away the sins of the entire world. So it was God himself who came to

---

[106] Ephesians 1:7–8
[107] 1 Peter 1:18–19

this world in the person of Jesus Christ to offer his precious blood as the payment to *redeem* you, to buy you back from death and hell.

I had to be sure to include that last verse above because it addresses one more common question and speaks to God's amazing love. Sometimes—alright, not sometimes—*all the time* people ask, "If God knew Adam and Eve were going to fall into sin, why didn't he stop them?" You know what my first answer is going to be.[108] But there are verses like the one above that clue us in on a decent answer. Here's how I like to say it:

> God is *so* amazing, *so* incredible, *so* powerful, *so* wise, *and so* loving that not only did he know in advance how they would ruin creation with sin, but he also knew how he would fix it!

Did you catch that at the end of those last verses? Peter said that Jesus was chosen even before the creation of the world to be the Lamb who would be slain to save sinners. It's like God knew every chess move and had Satan at checkmate before the game even began! That's how wise God is, how much God loves us, and that's how much God values you!

Can I throw in a couple more encouraging verses? The point is made already (I hope!) but sometimes it's good to have extra verses to go back to in tough times. Well here they are:

> Do not fear, for I have redeemed you . . . you are precious and honored in my sight.[109]

> [Jesus Christ] gave himself for us to redeem us from all wickedness and to purify for himself a people that are his very own, eager to do what is good.[110]

---

108 Add it to your list for heaven!

109 Isaiah 43:1, 4

110 Titus 2:14

Do you not know that your bodies are temples of the Holy Spirit, who is in you, whom you have received from God? You are not your own; you were bought at a price.[111]

But you are a chosen people, a royal priesthood, a holy nation, God's special possession, that you may declare the praises of him who called you out of darkness into his wonderful light.[112]

God has loved us so dearly and paid such an extraordinary price to redeem us from sin that now we are God's special possession as his own dear people. Peter is right! What else can we do but declare his praises?

If you ever feel worthless because of your sin and what you have done, and thus wonder if God would still love and value you, then know this important last fact:

Fact #3 – You are priceless because you have human life, because God uniquely made you to be you, and because *Jesus paid a price beyond any value for you* so that you could be God's dear possession now and forever.

Summary
In a sinful world that is no longer paradise, there are so many things and so many people that make us feel worthless. In addition to those who fail us in sin, haters gonna hate. Some will sinfully try to make you feel worthless on purpose. How pathetic!

But then there is the comparison game. As we look at the world around us through our eyes and through our phones and computers we quickly find that we don't live up to the imaginary standards the world sets in place. We're not as pretty, not as smart, not as athletic, not as popular. Again, we feel worthless.

---

[111] 1 Corinthians 6:19–20
[112] 1 Peter 2:9

Then there are the sad times when those who are supposed to love and care for us let us down. Yes, even parents, pastors, teachers, and friends can let us down and make us feel like we have no value. Suddenly you find yourself thinking, *I feel worthless.* That's when you need to focus on the facts.

Let's review them:

> Fact #1 – You are priceless because you have human life and God made human life to be sacred and special above all creatures.

> Fact #2 – You are priceless because God specially and specifically made you to be you.

> Fact #3 – You are priceless because God himself paid a price beyond value for you to be his own—he gave himself. Jesus redeemed you with his own life so that you would be his eternally.

This value, this worth in God's sight is all yours in Jesus. This is your identity. Just as the Father treasures his dear Son Jesus, so now he treasures you, his dear child. That's your identity. That's your status now and forever.

Speaking of forever, let's close by taking another sneak peek at eternity through the eyes and pen of John. In chapter 5, John records for us a special scene he saw in heaven. There he saw Jesus, the Lamb who was slain and that paid the price for us. Those in heaven were singing the praises of Jesus with this song:

> You are worthy . . .
> because you were slain,
>> and with your blood you purchased for God
>> persons from every tribe and language and people
>> and nation.[113]

---

113 Revelation 5:9

To this tens of thousands of angels erupted with praise, "Worthy is the Lamb, who was slain!"[114] And then every creature in heaven joined to give him praise and it was followed by a resounding "Amen!" as all fell down to worship our God.

Oh, to be there! Oh, to be there to thank and praise our God who personally values us so highly! Patience. One day soon we will!

Until then, dear teen, trust the facts. Trust God's words.

You *are* priceless!

---

[114] Revelation 5:12

Chapter 8

Feeling: I Feel Weak

vs.

Fact: I Am Strong

Everybody loved Larissa. Like *everybody*. If Captain Marvel, Wonder Woman, and Simone Biles were all combined into one person, that's how people viewed Larissa. She was supremely athletic—the star and captain for three different sports. Students and faculty alike loved watching her compete with such grace and class yet such jaw-dropping strength and speed. Younger girls even asked for her autograph after basketball games.

Larissa was so much more than an athletic standout though. She was a 4.0 student and in the academic top ten—with an overloaded schedule and extra AP classes. She was student body president and commanded attention and respect whenever she spoke or addressed the school. Yet Larissa never had to demand respect. It was her spunky personality, her huge pearly-white smile, and her contagious laugh that won people over quickly, and it was her commitment to helping others that made people adore her. Larissa was a leader at church, too. She was viewed as having a mature faith and helped run the summer Vacation Bible School program every year. And yes, of course, Larissa was drop-dead gorgeous. At least four freshmen boys saw her in the first week and believed the rumor that she was Beyoncé's cousin.

Larissa was respected and trusted by every teacher and school administrator. She was basically the face of the school. Students loved her and looked up to her and wanted to be like her. Even parents caught themselves slipping and saying things at times like, "How come you can't be more like Larissa?" To everyone, Larissa was the strongest student that had graced the hallways of that high school for decades.

But what no one knew—and no one would have ever guessed in a million years—was that Larissa was dying on the inside. At any particular moment Larissa felt like she was going to crumble and be exposed for a fraud.

See, she dominated in athletics, but no one saw how the drive for perfection and success and winning drove her crazy. There was always some athlete out there who was faster, stronger, or better. She was a force in the classroom too, but no one knew how hard she worked to scrape and claw for every last A. She only slept about three to four hours a night and lived on caffeine as she tried to find the stamina to keep up with all her homework. All the extra school responsibilities were a burden, too. No one denied that she was an incredible leader, but Larissa tried to deny how hard it was to juggle all the student council projects and events on top of everything else.

Those were the obvious burdens on Larissa that people could see, yet they had no idea how much she was struggling with all of it. However, there were even more secret things that Larissa kept bottled up.

She had been in a relationship with another stud athlete for over two years. They were *that* couple that made everyone go "Aww!" and "Give me a break!" at the same time because they were so perfect. No one knew though that they had been drifting apart. The relationship was fracturing. Communication was a disaster. They both knew it and wanted to fix it, yet they couldn't figure out how. Larissa was heartbroken and crushed that the end seemed near.

Then came the final punch that delivered the knockout blow. Larissa's grandma was one of her favorite people on earth. Aside from her parents, she loved no one as dearly as MeMa. She had done everything with her and shared everything with her since she was a little girl. Then one day the phone call came in. MeMa had a heart attack and was in the hospital.

Larissa's family rushed to the hospital to be by her side. For three days they watched and prayed fervently as her life started slipping away. And as Larissa watched her grandma's strength failing, she also she felt like the cracks in her armor were about to shatter.

And they did.

After MeMa died, Larissa had a total breakdown. She didn't think she could handle it anymore. It was all too much. School, homework, sports, leadership, friends, social life, boyfriend, and all the heartache of life—it was just too much. Everyone thought Larissa was the strongest student around—physically, emotionally, spiritually—but what no one knew was that Larissa couldn't get one thought out of her mind—*I feel so weak!*

Feeling Weak

What is it about weakness that is so terrifying? When we come into this world, weakness is natural to us. In fact, it's all you know. As a baby, you can't do much more besides cry and destroy your diaper with vomit-inducing smells, liquids, and solids. You depend on your parents, especially your mother, for everything—to be soothed, to be fed, to be clothed, to be changed into yet another diaper that you will yet again demolish. And you're OK with that. But there's something about humans that make them want their children to grow up to be tough and strong.

Now in one sense, this is understandable and even good. We want boys who will grow into men who selflessly care for and protect their wives and children. We want girls who will grow into elegant yet fierce women who can handle struggles in the home or out of it. This is true in almost every culture around the world.

Yet there is certainly a point where this desire for strength crosses the line. Emphasis on strength suddenly turns into a phobia of weakness, as if it's a disease to be avoided and eradicated from your life at all costs. So dads teach their boys things like, "Crying is for girls. Toughen up! Never show weakness!" Moms teach their girls similar things, as if any kind of gentleness, humility, or grace in a woman means you are some kind of second-class, weak-willed woman. Kids tease each other and call people "mama's boys" or "crybabies" or as they get older they just label people as "weak."

At the same time, we very much so live in an American culture that is built on the premises of self-help, hard work, and strength to achieve your personal goals and dreams. Who wants to look weak when you are competing for college scholarships and building your personal resume? Who wants to look weak when your parents have so many dreams and aspirations for your future? Who wants to look weak to the manager when a raise or promotion is at stake?

In such a cultural context, who would ever admit—*I feel weak?* This is a *big* problem, because the irony of it all is that we *are* weak.

It probably goes without saying that this chapter has nothing to do with muscle strength. You might be able to squat three plates on each side, or you might be able to bench jack squat. You might be able to dunk a basketball, or you might barely be able to dunk a donut. It doesn't matter because any person of any physical strength can still be or feel weak on the inside. That's what we're going to focus more of our attention on here—internal weakness.

The first area where we often feel weakness is emotionally. This is the kind of weakness that is felt when you are overwhelmed and overburdened by the struggling and suffering of everyday life. For every person this is different, so let's think about some of these areas of life that start to overwhelm us and cause us to be emotionally weak:

> Home. Teen life at home is just tough. Plain and simple. There's no way around that. It always has been and always will be. Parents struggle to understand their teens and teens struggle to understand their parents. Communication breaks down. There are arguments and fights, sometimes yelling and shouting. Usually tons of attitude. But then you add to the normal struggles of growing up the facts I've tossed at you before—how many families are missing a parent from the start or marriages that are crumbling and lead to divorce. As you are growing into adult type of thinking, you want and need support and strength at home. Sadly, I have worked with far too many teens who are completely overwhelmed by all the problems at home and with parents that they feel so weak.

> School. School is a beast. It's just one of those things that everyone has to do but is super-duper hard to get through. I get why seniors do the whole "senior slide" thing. There's some kind of light at the end of the tunnel and they just want to be done with it. What school has become today is extraordinarily stressful. There is constant pushing from parents and teachers to excel and exceed. There's endless competition among peers to get good grades and test scores and scholarship dollars. There are *way* too many AP classes and for some reason too many students think they are some kind of alien lifeform that can handle multiple AP classes at the same time in a healthy way. Then there's all the other activities—sports, music, drama, clubs, student council, etc. Everyone wants your time. Everyone demands your

best. Well, eventually everything piles up and becomes so overwhelming that you just can't handle it and you end up feeling so weak.[115]

Social life. This is a huge one, and it's really complicated, isn't it? In middle school there's some drama about how this person likes that person or that dude's voice is changing and sounds like a dying mouse. But nothing too bad. Freshmen year usually students enter high school full of excitement and hopes and dreams and a whole bunch of nervousness and fears. They're too young and inexperienced to get too deep into drama. But then everyone starts settling in and finds their friend groups and lots of dating goes on and so much more! Things get complicated fast between that sophomore-junior year. Then—and I'm often surprised by this—there is usually one more big incident of drama for some reason during senior year. Someone does something dumb and someone is stabbed in the back and it's the end of the world and things will never be the same (you know the kind of drama I'm talking about). This is a lot of emotional stress to endure! Home life and school life are hard enough, but when your social life is a mess, who has the strength to endure all that?

Social media. This has to be mentioned along with your social life because they often go hand in hand. So much of what you experience socially with friends, boyfriend/girlfriend, teammates, and classmates is

---

115 PRO TIP: FYI, Watch out for your sophomore-junior year transition. I have noticed that this is when things get really dicey. Your brains are just about fully into "abstract thinking" mode and you're looking at life differently. You are starting to get more freedoms as you and your friends are able to drive. BUT, classes and athletics are also getting much more tough and intense. The ACT is looming, and you figure out that colleges are looking at your junior year as a key year. AP tests are starting, and your future is creeping up on you. Watch out! Not only do I see students crack under this pressure, but I also see them cave in to temptations, too!

through social media. But that's complicated too. How do you keep up with all the messages? How do you respond to that one message—were they trying to be rude and mean or not? And why doesn't she respond to me—I can see that she read it at 8:31p.m. and the little typing bubble has been popping up for 10 minutes! Then there are all the pictures and photos that bring so much stress—keeping up with all the posts you need to like and comment on, wondering why nobody likes your recents, editing your pics and thinking up the perfect captions, seeing friends gathered together and wondering why no one invited you, and so much more. Managing your digital self is tough! It's like you have a whole different persona that you are trying to display to the world—some perfect, cooler version of yourself. This is hard to keep up with! All the social media stress can make a person feel so weak!

Dating. Yeah, we better talk about this one too. I know that all of you holding this book are in totally different places. Some of you don't care much about dating at all and haven't been too worried about it. You're rare, and I'm sure your parents are glad you might not date until you're 30. But it's OK. Don't sweat the dating stuff. But then there's the rest of you. Yikes. Teen dating is rough, isn't it? One minute she likes you and the next minute she doesn't. One week you're "talking to each other" and then the next week you're "talking-talking," and then, just when you think you're going to be officially dating, he starts talking to someone else![116] And then, oh then, there is the teenage romance. There are the times when

---

[116] OK, old guy check here. This is one thing I just don't get. I find this so confusing. How do you know when you're "talking" to someone because you're interested and flirting or when you're "talking-talking" like it's getting more serious or when you're actually dating or when you're just talking to someone because they are literally a human being standing in front of you that you are talking to? I am a much bigger fan of the '80s and '90s when you were friends, dating, or going steady. See how simple that is?!

you fall head over heels in love. This is when you start saying things like, "O – M – Goodness! This has been the best six months, four days, and eight seconds of my entire life. I will always love him/her forever and ever and I would just die without him/her." Umm. False. Sorry. These are the relationships that younger teens often have and they really sting when they end because it seems like life will end. But then last and most painful of all, there are the relationships that are actually very serious. These are the couples that date for one or two or more years. When these relationships end, the emotional toll is devastatingly heartbreaking. These are the "give me all my stuff back / I'm deleting all my pics of you / but only after I cry myself to sleep" types of relationships. Whether you haven't dated and hope to some day or you've dated more than you like to admit, the teen dating scene is enough to make anyone crumble, crack, and confess their weakness.

There are so many things that wear you down though, aren't there? Getting cut from a team. Missing the big shot. Messing up in the recital or the play in front of everyone. Gossip. You get the idea and you know all too well. Teen life is filled with things that make you feel emotionally weak.

Have you been in one of those weak spots before? Each person experiences these differently. For some it may be just a bad moment and they try to "shake it off" like Taylor Swift. Others find themselves in a funk, like an emotional ditch they fell into that they can't climb out of. But then there are others that get hit really hard with emotional stress. Life becomes overwhelming and too much to handle. "Why bother? Why keep going? What's the point? It's not going to get better. It just is what it is." Sometimes it may feel like you're carrying an elephant on your back—there's no way you can handle the burden and you feel like you're about to get crushed. You feel so weak.

Those moments can be very dangerous. It is very important to be emotionally and mentally healthy, and if you are feeling like you are struggling, it is important to talk to someone or even have professional help. But there is another reason emotional weakness is dangerous—it often can lead to spiritual weakness.

There are many different ways that your emotional stress and weakness might start to affect your spiritual life. Let's talk now about some of the reactions people have to the weaknesses of life:

Anger. Some people become angry with God. "How could you do this, God? Don't you care? What kind of a God lets this happen to his people?" Anger often leads people to push God away because they feel like he isn't helping them at all.

Doubt. Doubt is a very common reaction to hardship in life. It's just like the anger reaction, but a little less aggressive. This is when the questions start flooding through your brain. "Why is this happening? Is God really watching? Is he really a loving God? Does he really hear my prayers? Will he really work things out for my good?"

Laziness. Some people become so overwhelmed with and caught up in the stress and emotional struggles of everyday life that they start slipping away from God. They aren't really angry with him. They don't really doubt him. But they definitely don't go to God. Prayers are few and far between. Church attendance is slim to none. The Bible stays constantly closed. Before you know it, this person feels extra weak because they are less connected to God than ever before.

Acting out. Once again, acting out shows up as a symptom for handling the many stressors of life. I'm going to keep bringing it up because I see it all the time.

Life becomes so worrisome and so stressful that teens start looking for ways to make themselves feel better. Drinking, drugs, and sex are just some of the ways that teens try to cope with their weaknesses. It makes them feel strong to do something rebellious and risky and "cool." At the same time, it feels good, and it helps them forget about the problems. What few people ever tell teens though is that after your rebellious moment of doing some of this stuff, you are going to crash. Your "high" of good feelings is gone, you will feel guilty about what you did, *and* surprise, surprise—your problems and weakness are still there!

The devil is no dummy. He knows when you are struggling. That's when he starts licking his chops and prepares to pounce on his prey—you! He knows full well that if you are feeling emotional weakness it won't be hard to lead you toward spiritual weakness.

And that leads us to one more thought about spiritual weakness. We also need to talk about our daily struggles with temptations and sins. You may be emotionally tough, and you may handle troubles in life with great emotional strength. However, no matter who you are, you are still going to be bombarded with temptations day after day. And oh my, the struggle is real!

I think one of the best illustrations of this is in the Garden of Gethsemane. Jesus is inching his way toward horrific moments of unthinkable suffering. He's true God. He knows what's coming—the betrayal, the arrest, the trials, the beatings, the mocking, the blood, the sin of the world on his shoulders. His emotional anguish was boiling over. So there in the quiet of the Garden he went away to pray. Jesus told his three closest friends, "My soul is overwhelmed with sorrow to the point of death. Stay here and keep watch with me."[117]

---

[117] Matthew 26:38

But as he went away to pray, not once, not twice, but three times he came back and found his closest friends sleeping. Were they that thickheaded? Were they that clueless? Could they really not tell that something big was about to go down? Did they not have any decency as friends that they would try at least a little harder to stay awake to keep watch and pray with Jesus?

It's in that context that Jesus spoke the following profound words that strike us right to our very core: "Watch and pray so that you will not fall into temptation. The spirit is willing, but the flesh is weak."[118] How true! And how painful! Jesus is reminding us that we need to be on our guard continually and prayerfully as we watch out for temptations that will come our way. Why? Because our spirit—our life of faith in him—might be willing, but our sinful flesh is very weak. Ain't that the truth?!

How many times have you given yourself a pep talk like you're Vince Lombardi trying to pump up the team? "You can do it! You can do it! You're not going to sin this time! You're not going to look at those websites! . . . You're not going to blow up with anger! . . . You're not going to drink at the party! . . . You're not going to treat your parents like dirt! . . . You're not going to cheat!" But next thing you know, there you are falling into that same old sin again. You know your triggers. You know the warning signs. You can see it coming from a mile away. Then, BOOM! Before you know it, you've fallen again.

Sometimes Satan really has us trapped though. Sometimes we are so spiritually weak that we even start to enjoy sin. We aren't on our spiritual guard at all and the sinning happens so fast and easily—the bad words come pouring out, the dirty jokes fly across the lunch table, the anger erupts in a flash, the lust fills our hearts. Everyone in church sees you and thinks you're just another "fine young Christian," but secretly you indulge in sin like a kid in a candy store. All the while the hidden feelings of spiritual weakness are eating away at your heart.

---

[118] Matthew 26:41

That's a rough place to be because it almost feels like you're having a UFC cage match in your own brain. The apostle Paul knew what that was like. He wrote about it extensively in Romans 7. What he describes there is the inner battle that he faced on a daily basis, the battle between his new life in Christ (his Holy Spirit-led life) and his sinful flesh. Listen to how he describes it and see if this doesn't sound and feel familiar:[119]

> I do not understand what I do. For what I want to do I do not do, but what I hate I do. And if I do what I do not want to do, I agree that the law is good. As it is, it is no longer I myself who do it, but it is sin living in me. For I know that good itself does not dwell in me, that is, in my sinful nature. For I have the desire to do what is good, but I cannot carry it out. For I do not do the good I want to do, but the evil I do not want to do—this I keep on doing. Now if I do what I do not want to do, it is no longer I who do it, but it is sin living in me that does it.[120]

Paul felt like he was going crazy! All the good things he wanted to do sincerely as a Christian, he found that he didn't do. And all the bad things that he didn't want to do that were sins, those he ended up doing anyways! His sinful heart kept playing the spiritual Uno-Reverse Card, but his heart of faith hated it! This weakness was eating him up on the inside so much that finally he just stopped what he was saying and erupted with these words:

> What a wretched man I am! Who will rescue me from this body that is subject to death?[121]

---

[119] Cool Bible note: Paul was a *brilliant* writer. Notice in some of these sentences how they even sound confusing. Paul wrote in this back-and-forth confusing kind of way to illustrate through his writing the inner turmoil and confusion of the fight he was experiencing. Clever!

[120] Romans 7:15–20

[121] Romans 7:24

Have you felt that way? Have you felt overwhelmed by things that are going on in your life? Is home too much? School? Homework? Have you been burdened by all the drama of friends or dating relationships or social media nonsense? Does it feel like it is too much to handle?

Or have you been so overwhelmed by temptations and sins? You try and you try. You want to be the kind of Christian that God wants you to be, but you just can't. You fail. You fall. You sin. Again and again.

These emotional and spiritual burdens can feel so heavy, like the weight of the world is crushing and suffocating us. It makes us want to burst out like the apostle Paul—*I feel so weak!*

When I feel like this, I need something different. I need some facts . . .

Fact: I Am Strong

What. Just. Happened??!! With dropped jaws and shaking knees they stared at each other in amazement. They were too in awe to even think about their clothes that were still soaked. It was one of those surreal moments that seemed to be real life but felt more like a dream. Did he just do what I think he did?

Moments before that they were terrified. A furious storm had broken out. The winds were ripping across the waters and the waves were pouring into the boat. You know when a group that has experienced fishermen in the boat is terrified, then it must be a bad storm. Terrified indeed. They couldn't bail the water fast enough. They were going down and likely about to drown. All they could think of was to turn to the person who had done all kinds of crazy amazing things before. Maybe he could do something. Anything would help!

But there was Jesus—fast asleep. Are. You. Kidding me? Asleep? "Teacher, don't you care if we drown?"[122]

---

[122] Mark 4:38

I wonder what Jesus in his human nature thought at that moment. As true God, he knew what was going down and he knew what he was about to do. But as true man, what was he thinking? Did he just smile? Did he roll his eyes a little bit? Amazingly, what Jesus didn't do was get up and rebuke his foolish disciples. Instead, shockingly, "He got up, rebuked the wind and said to the waves, 'Quiet! Be still!'"[123]

What? Who does that? What kind of crazy dude talks to storms? And how is it possible that it stopped? It didn't lighten up to a drizzle. It didn't pass by in a few minutes. The storm stopped dead in its tracks in that moment and it was completely calm.

"They were terrified and asked each other, 'Who is this? Even the wind and the waves obey him!'"[124] This wasn't the first time and it wouldn't be the last time that the disciples were so in awe of Jesus' strength that they were afraid to be in his presence. They just didn't get it quite yet. But soon enough they would.

Have you had these kinds of moments in your life? Moments when you have felt completely helpless and hopeless, so weak that there is absolutely nothing you can possibly do to make it better? Have you wanted to cry out to God like these disciples did, "Lord, don't you care? I'm drowning here! I don't have the strength to do this!"

That's what makes Jesus' miracles so special. Little by little, as if a door was cracking open slowly, Jesus had these miraculous moments that gave glimpses of who he really is. They were always shocking. Like seriously, who makes the paralyzed to walk or the blind to see? But in the more spectacular miracles when Jesus opened the door a bit wider—like calming the storm or showing his glory at his transfiguration—the disciples quickly became afraid. His divine might and strength as true God were almost too much for them.

---

[123] Mark 4:39
[124] Mark 4:41

Realize what Jesus was doing though. With each of these miracles Jesus was reinforcing his message. He was pointing to himself with a giant LED-lit arrow that said, "See! I *am* the One. I *am* the promised Messiah that everyone is looking for. I *am* sent from God. I *am* God."

If you think about it, Jesus' entire life was miraculous from beginning to end:

> He was conceived without a human father by the Holy Spirit and born of a virgin.

> He lived a perfect life with no sins. Ever. Not one sin one time. He perfectly defeated every temptation of Satan. Yet not only did he avoid sin, but he also loved his heavenly Father and all people perfectly. In other words, he was perfect both in what he did and didn't do.

> He suffered immeasurable human pain. The beatings and flogging and crown of thorns could have led to the death of any normal human. Crucifixion was a horrible way to suffer as slowly the lungs would collapse and eventually the person would suffocate. On top of all that suffering, Jesus carried the weight of the sin and guilt of the entire world. I can barely handle my own, yet Jesus carried the sin of every person ever. And all this was while he was abandoned by his heavenly Father so that he could suffer hell for us. Yet not only did Jesus not cave in and sin during this suffering, but he also accomplished the mission. He crushed Satan at the cross and declared his mighty victory as he proclaimed, "It is finished!"[125]

> He rose from the dead. I suppose some person along the way could have been loving enough to say, "I would like to die for the sins of the world to save them." That might be nice, but fat chance of that working. It

---

[125] John 19:30

wouldn't be a perfect life, the death wouldn't be powerful enough to pay for sin, *and* that person would stay dead. So how would we even know if the plan ever worked? This is *not* the case with Jesus. Death and hell couldn't hold our Savior. He proved his victory with his empty tomb and then proved that he was alive to hundreds of people.

He ascended into heaven. In his last moments visibly on earth, Jesus triumphantly ascended into the clouds and disappeared as he gave two awesome statements of promise and power: "All authority in heaven and on earth has been given to me . . . And surely I am with you always, to the very end of the age."[126]

Every single moment of Jesus' earthly life was filled with divine strength that we cannot comprehend. I think that's what makes that scene in the Garden of Gethsemane especially profound. Remember those words we just reviewed? Jesus said, "The spirit is willing, but the flesh is weak."[127] That is *so* true for us. We are so very weak even when we may be wishing or willing to be strong. But not so with Jesus. The very person who spoke those words then went on within the next three days to prove at the cross and the empty tomb just how strong he is.

But here's the best part. This is not just some distant God who is strong and mighty, but we are left wondering if he might ever help us. Not at all! As we have reviewed so far, this is a loving and gracious God who cares deeply about you personally. Therefore, his strength becomes your strength! Listen to these comforting words of Isaiah:

> Do you not know?
>   Have you not heard?
> The LORD is the everlasting God,

---

[126] Matthew 28:18, 20
[127] Matthew 26:41

the Creator of the ends of the earth.
He will not grow tired or weary,
    and his understanding no one can fathom.
He gives strength to the weary
    and increases the power of the weak.
Even youths grow tired and weary,
    and young men stumble and fall;
but those who hope in the LORD
    will renew their strength.
They will soar on wings like eagles;
    they will run and not grow weary,
    they will walk and not be faint.[128]

Incredible! The everlasting and almighty God who made heaven and earth, who performed mighty wonders, who came in human flesh, who had the power to calm the winds and the waves, who crushed Satan and defeated death—that God will give strength to the weary and power to the weak. Yes, even youths and teens who can grow tired and weary—God will give them strength, too. Your strength will be renewed so that with God you will soar like an eagle through all the troubles of life.

This is God's promise to you. Listen to his own words in the next chapter of Isaiah:

So do not fear, for I am with you;
    do not be dismayed, for I am your God.
I will strengthen you and help you;
    I will uphold you with my righteous right hand.[129]

It's not just about feeling weak. We *are* weak. But God is anything but that. When we see his strength and hear his promises about giving us strength, that is what will fill our hearts with courage to be confident in our God. Look at how some of God's people of old burst out in confidence:

---

[128] Isaiah 40:28–31
[129] Isaiah 41:10

The LORD is my strength and my defense;
he has become my salvation.
He is my God, and I will praise him,
my father's God, and I will exalt him.[130]

Be strong and courageous. Do not be afraid; do not be
discouraged, for the LORD your God will be with you
wherever you go.[131]

My flesh and my heart may fail,
but God is the strength of my heart
and my portion forever.[132]

This is your confidence. This is your strength. It's God's
strength! This is also our first fact:

Fact #1 – You *are strong*. You are strong because God is
strong. His almighty power is seen in everything from
his creation to your salvation in Jesus Christ. Your
gracious God promises to give you that strength to
uphold you when you are weak.

But what about? . . .

Satan is such a jerk face. Here we have these amazing facts about
God's strength, particularly as seen in the works of Jesus, and
then we have these amazing promises from God about how he
will strengthen us. Incredible! But then Satan has to go and do
his thing and try and ruin everything by whispering doubts into

---

[130] Exodus 15:2. This is from the famous Song of Moses which the Israelites
sang when God delivered them through the Red Sea from the Egyptians.
Read the whole song! It is filled with comfort about God's mighty strength.
And by the way, this event is a foreshadow of how God would later deliver us
through the waters of baptism from our enemies of sin and Satan and lead us
on to the Promised Land of heaven. Now there's some strength!
[131] Joshua 1:9
[132] Psalm 73:26

our ears, things that will try to get us to focus on our feelings of weakness. Yup. Jerk face.

Yet we dare not minimize or make light of these traps. They are dangerous! Do you know these thoughts?

> But what about when dad loses his job? . . .

> But what about when dad and mom get divorced? . . .

> But what about when I break a leg and my sports career is finished? . . .

> But what about when I get a 2 on the AP and I wasted my semester and lost out on thousands of dollars? . . .

> But what about when mom suddenly dies? . . .

> But what about when I get cancer? . . .

> But what about when *you fill in the blank*? . . .

Satan knows that you know about God's strength. God's words and what Jesus said and did are plain as day. He can't deny those things. What Satan can do, though, is try to insert a big BUT into your thinking. "*But* what if that doesn't apply to me," or, "*But* what if that doesn't apply to this situation," or, "*But* what if it's not enough for this situation." Yup. Jerk face. Here's a general rule of thumb for you for life. This is good old-guy advice: Don't listen to a jerk face. Especially when it's Satan. Instead, listen to God.

When these questions flood your thinking, this is the perfect time to turn to the famous words of the apostle Paul in Philippians: "I can do all this through him who gives me strength."[133]

---

133 Philippians 4:13

We need to talk about this verse. It is one of the most comforting verses in the Bible, and yet at the same time it is one of the most misunderstood verses in the Bible. The verse has been popularized in American Christianity and made its way onto home decorations and plaques, window clings, and tattoos. It's been seen by millions on the shoes of Stephen Curry and the eye black of former college star QB Tim Tebow.

However, the way this verse has been used is a little misleading. The way many talk about this verse is that they can do anything *earthly* with God's strength. So if you have big enough dreams and work hard enough, you can win a championship like Tim Tebow or Steph Curry with God's strength. Now while it's true that God does give talents and abilities to everyone, it is not as though God randomly gives super strength to one person and not to the other. Think about it this way: Are we to believe that Steph Curry can do everything with God's strength, but the players on the losing team can't?

Let's be more practical. Let's say two people have stage three cancer. For both it is looking grim. Both have families that rally around their loved one and make T-shirts that say, "I can do all this through him who gives me strength." But then let's say that one dies from cancer and the other has a remarkable comeback, goes into remission, and is now cancer free. Should we believe that God gives strength to some people but not to other people? Or should we think that God's strength only works some of the time? Or maybe God's strength isn't all that it's cracked up to be? This is the problem with how people often understand this verse.

Thus, the key to understanding this verse is first in understanding that it's worded poorly in English.[134] How it's worded in most Bibles is a little misleading. A little better translation in English would be something like this:

---

[134] Did you know the New Testament was written originally in Greek?

In all things I am strong in the one who strengthens me.

You see the real point of this awesome verse is *not* that God will give you the strength to do anything you want. The point of the verse is that in all things—all situations, all problems, all troubles—God will give you the strength to endure it. Now that's real comfort!

Let's say you have the most devastating breakup imaginable. God will not necessarily give you the strength to patch it back up and get back together with Mr./Ms. Dreamy. But he *will* give you the strength to get through the heartbreak, to learn from it, and to move on with your life.

Let's say you have every bit of school stress imaginable. You have three AP classes and two honors classes. It's getting to be time for all the big tests. The pressure is mounting to achieve and accomplish. God will not necessarily give you the strength to get a perfect score on every test and get every scholarship you ever wanted. But he *will* give you the strength to handle the outcomes—no matter how well or poorly you did on the tests and no matter what scholarships you do or do not receive.

Or finally, let's take it to an extreme and say that you get diagnosed with cancer. God will not necessarily give you the strength to beat the cancer and become cancer free. But God *will* give you the strength to endure all the sadness, sickness, and struggles that come with cancer.

In all of these situations, God can certainly do anything he sees fit. He can answer your prayers and help you in big ways. But God might also see something else as best for your life. The point is that regardless of the situation or outcome, God will give you strength to endure it. That brings us to our next fact guaranteed by God's Word:

Fact #2 – You *are strong* because God is strong and he promises to give you that strength *in any and every situation*. God's strength is something that he has promised to give you for all things that you go through in life.

Great! Awesome! Amazing! God promises his strength in all things! Ugh . . . here comes that jerk face again.

> But what if I breakup with someone and never have a relationship again? What kind of strength is that?

> But what if I have people that sinfully torment me and mock me and bully me and I can endure it, but they never ever stop. Isn't enough finally enough for a person?

> But what if I get cancer and God gives strength to endure all the tough times that come with it, but then I die? That's strength?

The next trick Satan has up his sleeve is to lead you to think like this, "OK. Fine. I have God's strength. But that's not really the kind of strength I was looking for. That's not good enough for me."

Super missionary Paul had a situation like this. Talk about someone who knew God's strength! He saw it in his personal faith life as God brought him from the clutches of the devil and unbelief to faith and trust in him. He saw it on his missionary journeys as various miracles were performed and thousands came to faith. He saw it as he endured fierce and painful persecution. He knew God's strength (He's even the guy that wrote the Philippians 4:13 verse, remember?). But was it all enough?

This is the question that Satan planted in his mind as Paul wrestled with something he called "his thorn in the flesh." What was this? We don't know. We have good guesses that it could have been constant battles with malaria or arthritis. It could've been really bad eyesight which he indicates in several letters (Maybe this was from malaria?). It also could have been a person that gave him non-stop ministry trouble. It's probably better that we don't know so we can apply his words to our own lives. Whatever it may have been, listen to his pain here:

> I was given a thorn in my flesh, a messenger of Satan, to torment me. Three times I pleaded with the Lord to take it away from me.[135]

Can you picture Paul in a low moment, begging in prayer for God to end his troubles and take away this "thorn," whatever it was? Have you been there before? Perhaps you have been the one begging God in your worst moments, "Please, Lord! Take this away! Make it better! Fix it! I feel so weak!" Listen to God's response to Paul and to you. Soak up every word and treasure what God says here:

> But he said to me, "My grace is sufficient for you, for my power is made perfect in weakness."[136]

God's response is so humbling. We often have this human vision of how our lives are supposed to play out. We imagine this fairytale of a life with the perfect family and job and amount of money and no sickness or problems. When we do have struggles, sometimes really awful ones, we beg God to take them away. That's when this reminder from the Lord is so critically important. You have what you need. You don't need your health. You don't need lots of money and a big house. You don't need everything in your life to work out like a Disney movie. But what you do need is God's grace. You need his undeserved love and forgiveness in Jesus Christ. You need the doors of heaven to be open to you so that you can enter a place

---

[135] 2 Corinthians 12:7–8
[136] 2 Corinthians 12:9

that is perfect with no pains or problems. And that you do have—now and forever. Thus, we can join Paul to go on to say this:

> Therefore I will boast all the more gladly about my weaknesses, so that Christ's power may rest on me. That is why, for Christ's sake, I delight in weaknesses, in insults, in hardships, in persecutions, in difficulties. For when I am weak, then I am strong.[137]

How's that for a mind-blowing perspective? That's a thought that no one in this world could possibly understand *unless* they have faith. That's right, you can actually boast in your weakness. You can be proud that you are human and that you can't do it all and that you can't endure it all on your own. Why? Because when you know you are weak, then you can know Christ's strength. And when you have Christ's strength, there is nothing more that you could ever ask for. You have the strength to overcome Satan, death, and hell. Christ has that strength and proved that strength, and that strength is now yours. Talk about a *strong* third fact!

> **Fact #3** – You *are strong* because God is strong. He has proven the facts of his strength in creation and in Jesus' victory. God promises to give you that strength in all situations. And best of all, you are strong because *you have God's grace* in Christ Jesus and there is nothing more we could possibly need to get through life in this world.

Summary
We live in a world that is constantly talking about strength. There are world record weight-lifters and muscle-bound modeling competitions. There are people who boast in their strength to achieve and people who overcome impossible odds.

---

[137] 2 Corinthians 12:9–10

The expectation is that you must be strong on your own. You must get through everything and figure it out by yourself. Otherwise, you are weak.

The problem is, no one can really handle all the stresses and struggles of everyday life on their own. Not teens, not even veteran adults. Endless things try us emotionally and make us feel emotionally weak. Then you add jerk face Satan into the mix and he constantly wants to prey on you to make you feel spiritually weak. There are countless times that any one of us might want to burst out and scream—*I feel so weak!* That's when you need to focus on the facts.

Let's review them:

> Fact #1 – You are strong because you have an all-powerful God who made all things and won the ultimate victory at the cross and empty tomb. That all-powerful God promises to give you that strength.

> Fact #2 – You are strong because your all-powerful God gives you that strength at all times and in all things.

> Fact #3 – You are strong because your all-powerful God will always give you exactly what you need to endure all things. Not worldly success. That comes and goes and finally doesn't last. Even better than that, God gives you his grace. That is sufficient.

We can think back to Paul when he was having that inner cage match, wrestling with his personal thoughts. He felt so weak because he felt like he kept losing to his sinful nature. We know those feelings! Yet listen to Paul's reminder:

> Thanks be to God! He gives us the victory through our Lord Jesus Christ.[138]

---

[138] 1 Corinthians 15:57

This is the epitome of understanding your new identity in Christ. It's knowing that you can't. It's knowing that you didn't and that you won't. Yet it's also knowing that *Jesus did* and because he did, *so did you.* Jesus won the victory, so you won the victory. Jesus has the strength, so you have the strength—now and forever.

Speaking of forever, we return to our previews of heaven with the apostle John. Do you recall that vision we reviewed where John saw all the people in heaven dressed in white robes and washed in the blood of the Lamb? In that same scene, listen to the song that the angels in heaven were singing:

> Amen!
> Praise and glory
> and wisdom and thanks and honor
> and *power and strength*
> be to our God for ever and ever.
> Amen![139]

The angels were singing praise to God for all that he is and has done, which includes his great power and strength. And what evidence, what *facts,* about his strength could be more clear than what he was able to accomplish? The Lamb who was slain defeated our enemy Satan and he made guilty sinners into innocent saints. He rescued people from the depths of hell and brought them to the heights of heaven.

What joys await us there! Want to know why God's grace is sufficient and all we need to make us strong? Look at this description of believers in heaven as that chapter closes:

> "they are before the throne of God
>   and serve him day and night in his temple;
> and he who sits on the throne
>   will shelter them with his presence.
> 'Never again will they hunger;

---

[139] Revelation 7:12 (emphasis added)

never again will they thirst.
The sun will not beat down on them,'
    nor any scorching heat.
For the Lamb at the center of the throne
    will be their shepherd;
'he will lead them to springs of living water.'
'And God will wipe away every tear from their eyes.'"[140]

Do you see it? Do you see the strength and might and majesty of the Lamb, Jesus Christ? Do you see what he has accomplished? He has reopened perfect paradise! That strength is your strength in Christ. That paradise is your paradise in Christ.

Dear teen, trust the facts. Trust God's words.

You *are* strong!

---

[140] Revelation 7:15–17

Chapter 9

Feeling: I Feel Alone

vs.

Fact: I Am Connected

Caleb was your average everyday kind of teenager. He looked like other teens. He acted like other teens. He enjoyed the things that teens enjoyed. Caleb was a part of the football team. Not a star, but he contributed. He was an honor roll student. He was on student council. He was a member at the local church that his family had been members at for years. Everything was "normal" for Caleb. Or so it would seem.

For Caleb, everything was too normal—so normal that he totally blended into the crowd. Sometimes he wondered if people ever noticed that he was there. In class, he wasn't the kid that was causing trouble and talking out of turn or the kid that was non-stop flirting or the kid who always raised his hand and did the "Ooh! Ooh! Me! Me!" thing. He was just there. In football, he rarely touched the ball. The other receiver got all the passes. He was hardly ever mentioned in practice, and one of the coaches kept calling him by his older brother's name. Did they really know who he was?

When it came to student council, Caleb didn't like it much at all. If he was honest, he would admit he did it just because his parents had made him join and the guidance counselor said it was good for his college resume. He never said much. He was only on one committee, but control-freak Francis and try-hard Harper did all the work. They barely even remembered to add him to the Google Doc after they had already done all the work.

But this was Caleb's life. It was so "normal" that he faded into the background like he was hiding in plain sight. He wasn't the star athlete. He couldn't sing. He would hang with people but wasn't part of the cool crowd. He had one girlfriend once for about a month, but no one else seemed very interested. It was almost like Caleb was living in his own little world and no one knew it.

Over time, this started to eat away at Caleb on the inside. He almost became paranoid about it. When he was in the cafeteria he always froze for a moment. Should he sit by himself? Should he sit with football teammates? Should he sit by the guys who used to be his friends but now moved on to be with the party people? He felt awkward and unnoticed every day at lunch.

The same is true with football. Should he just quit? Would the team care? Would the coaches care? Was he really needed? What if he just quit school, too? There are good jobs out there. He could finish his degree online. It's not like he was missing out on his social life! Caleb was pretty convinced he wouldn't talk to anyone after graduation anyways.

All these thoughts would have been a little easier for Caleb if things were better at home. But they weren't. It's not that his parents didn't care about him. They did, or at least Caleb was *pretty sure* they did. The problem was that he never saw them. Caleb's dad worked the second shift, so he was normally gone when Caleb came home from school. His mom was a nurse and always worked overtime trying to make extra money to make ends meet, as she explained. But they were workaholics. They worked all the time, rarely took vacations, and just zoned out to Candy Crush on their old iPhones when they were home. Since Caleb's brother moved out of the house, Caleb almost never saw anyone at home, let alone talked to anyone.

Because the family was so consumed with work that meant the family fell into some bad habits with church. Little by little over the years they had been attending less and less. They weren't quite ChrEaster Christians,[141] but they were getting close. Caleb used to enjoy church and teen group, but now he just figured it was yet another place where no one would notice him.

How did it get to be like this? It was kind of a gradual thing over time. The thought finally occurred to Caleb though—he had no one. His family was never there. He didn't really have any best friends. He didn't have a girlfriend. He hardly went to church anymore. He felt so disconnected from other people, and even worse, so disconnected from God. He couldn't help but have a continual thought run through his head—*I feel so alone.*

Feeling Alone

It's the strangest thing, isn't it? How can it possibly be that in a world where we are so connected that at the exact same time we can be so disconnected? Have you noticed this? I bet you have even if you haven't thought about it. I'll give you some examples from my life.

In the last three years I have traveled to or through about 25 states by car. I've also been to Montana, California, Alaska, Antigua, and London, and each of those trips were with my wife and two kids who were still in elementary or middle school. My wife and I have also been to Zambia, Zimbabwe, and Dubai in the last three years. In the last few weeks I've communicated with people from Toronto, Paraguay, Brazil, Mexico, and Ukraine. Just yesterday I messaged with one of my friends from the island of Antigua. I regularly text with people from California, Texas, Florida, and many other places.

Who could have imagined 30 or more years ago that the world would be so connected? You can travel anywhere in the globe in less time and for less money than ever before. You can email

---

[141] Christians who only go to church on Christmas and Easter.

with someone at your school, text with someone across the country, and WhatsApp video chat with someone on the other side of the planet—and you could even do all those things simultaneously! Personally, I think this is fantastic, and it's one of the things I love the most about modern day living.

However, despite all these digital connections, people are perhaps more *dis*connected than ever before. My family had dinner at a restaurant not too long ago. Another family of four sat next to us. It caught our attention after a while that the entire time they sat there not one person spoke a word to or even looked at another person in their family. Mom and dad were on their phones and the kids were glued to their tablets. Our family had a good laugh about it . . . until we considered that we aren't always much better. When we go on road trips the kids want to watch movies in the van or play on a device. When we are at home we usually default to watching TV as a family . . . except my son wants to be on his phone, my daughter on an iPad, and my wife and I are doing work (OK, or playing too) on our phones or iPads—all while we are "watching" a show.

Do you realize how normal this is? Just look around your school sometime to observe the behaviors of other students (yes, and teachers!). It won't take long to see it. Every sporting event has stands that are filled with people staring at their phones and paying zero attention to the game. At those schools that allow phones during the day, kids rarely look up from their phones to look at other students. After school there are people making their way around the school campus bumping into others and walls and doorways because their focus is fixed on a screen. We're so connected, yet we are so disconnected.

We aren't only disconnected when we are together though. You might argue that you are "talking" to people through technology, but even though you are "connecting" with people digitally or virtually, you have to ask yourself whether those are quality conversations or relationships. You shoot out brief and sometimes incomplete sentences at random times in text messages. Then you read into the messages you receive something that is totally wrong, and you miscommunicate because it's just plain text and you don't really know how the other person feels. Sometimes you don't even send words as it's just a series of random emojis or GIFs. You also talk through FaceTime, but even then you're probably doing something else and not even looking at the other person. We have all these ways to connect with people and yet none of them facilitate real, quality communication.

Let's think about this for a second then. You don't look at people face to face. You don't talk face to face. You communicate in a bunch of short and random messages or pictures or smiley faces. You do most of this from the isolation of your home or your bedroom. I have to ask the question— How connected are you actually?

This is why I hate to say it—sorry, my dear teens—but you are really bad at conversations.[142] We adults are guilty of all this, too. 100%. But you teens have grown up this way. This kind of digital, virtual life is all you know, and that fact is exposed all the time. I have had thousands of conversations with teens and every time we have a good conversation or a deep talk, or even a small group face-to-face Bible study, nearly every time the teens have been very moved by it. Nearly all of them explain that they simply are not used to that level of conversation. I'll give you a real-life example.

Not long ago I took a mission team to California to work with a church near San Diego. Every evening when it was time to relax we would sit around the fire at the pastor's house and just talk. Nothing formal, just straight talk. Well one conversation led to another and the teens started opening up and expressing how they feel and asking tough Bible questions that were on their minds and talking about problems that they go through. Before we knew it, we were up talking almost every night for multiple

---

[142] #sorrynotsorry

hours and usually past midnight. All seven teens who went on the trip later expressed how touched they were by those talks. A number of them explained that it was because they had never really talked to other people in that way before. They had never felt so *connected*.

So this is my first point for you, my teen friend. Do a little double check on your digital life. Don't be so foolish or naïve as to think, "I talk to my friends all the time when I'm playing video games or on Snapchat or by text." I know you're smarter than that! Think critically about how much you are staring at a TV or phone or tablet. Think carefully about how screen time and technology might interfere with how much and how well you communicate with your family, your friends, or your boyfriend/girlfriend. Technology can be a great blessing, but before you know it you will be the next modern-day teen that is connected to the world yet at the same time can't stop thinking: *I feel so alone!*

Now that I finished my techie-sermon, it's time to do a little more thinking about feeling alone. When you have those feelings, it's also important to understand why (besides blaming technology). What has led to you feeling alone? Whom do you feel that you are *not* connecting with so that you do feel alone?

I'm going to keep this simple and easy to remember for you. Whom do you need to connect with? God and other people. I know that sounds like a cheap Sunday School type of answer, but it really is that simple. Let's explore those two areas and what may contribute to feeling alone and disconnected from God and from others.

It's probably best for us to go back to the beginning again, as in Genesis and "the" beginning. We've already talked quite a bit about creation and the fall into sin, so let's just review quickly. Remember that even in a perfect world that was free from sin God noted that it was not good for man to be alone.[143] So God

---

[143] Genesis 2:18

made Eve and instituted marriage and gave the blessing of families. God wanted humans to be connected with other people. When God finished with his creation and everything was perfectly "good," so also were relationships. Adam and Eve had perfect relationships and connections in two aspects— horizontally and vertically. Their relationship with each other was perfect, and their relationship with God was perfect.

Then came sin. As always, sin ruins what was perfect.

Think one more time about the first things that Adam and Eve did after they sinned. First, they covered themselves up because they were ashamed. They weren't comfortable with who they were or with each other. And next, they hid. They weren't comfortable in their relationship with God. This was exposed even more in the conversation with God that followed.[144] What did Adam do when God came and asked him where he was and what happened? He made excuses, lied, and passed the blame onto Eve. His words and actions showed that the relationship he had with God and with Eve were both fractured.

Understand this first then—we struggle in our relationships and often feel lonely *because of sin.* Sin is what causes deep hurt in our relationships with God and with others. Let's explore how this happens.

Sin separates you from God.[145] It's hard to hear, but it makes sense. When you do what is unholy and wrong, it separates you from the God who is holy and righteous. Or in other words, how can sinners hang with the one who is sinless? Now Jesus has restored that relationship and reconnected us,[146] but sin still does damage while we are living on this side of heaven.

---

[144] Genesis 3:9–13

[145] Isaiah 59:2

[146] *Lots* more on this to come so please keep reading to get to the super awesome Jesus stuff of this chapter!

Guess who's behind that? Here we go again . . . Satan. The one who accuses is so eager to do just that. He wants you to feel guilty about your sin. He wants you to feel ashamed and embarrassed like Adam and Eve did in the Garden. He wants you to feel like God would never love you after what you've done. He wants you to feel like your other problems in life are more important. The devil uses all these things to chisel away at your faith, hoping that with enough cracks he might shatter your relationship with God. Think about some of the ways Satan tries to lead you away from God.

> Blame. Just like Adam blamed God ("You gave me that woman!"), so we sometimes blame God for our problems or even our sins. "You never should have had me in that situation in the first place, Lord." But when we blame God, we push him away.

> Anger. I know a man who left my church and nearly gave up on his faith because he was so angry that his wife had died from cancer. He felt that God didn't help him, so he didn't need God. Notice how being angry with God usually goes hand in hand with blaming God. Once again, this is pushing God away.

> Acting out. Here acting out makes its way into our conversation once more. The devil wants you to act out in sin because it's cool and you're young and thus it's no big deal. Or he wants you to think that you've already done some stuff so you might as well keep on sinning. The more we chase down the path of sin though, the further we stray from God's path and God himself.

> Guilt. Like Adam and Eve trying to hide from God, our guilt sometimes makes us feel like we need to stay away from such a holy God. I once talked with a man who hadn't come to our church for ages. He told me, "Pastor, I'm afraid if I come to worship the church will cave in on me." That was partial excuse, but that was also guilt.

He didn't feel worthy enough for God, so he pushed him away.

Laziness. This one reveals what a sneaky snake that devil is with us. It's hard to see spiritual laziness creeping up on you until you're in way over your head. Little by little you pray less, you read your Bible less, you go to church less. Before you know it, you hardly do anything to feed your faith. Gradually over time and in your laziness, you have slowly pushed God out of your life.

Notice how *none* of these things involve *God* pushing you away. God never leaves you and takes away his presence, power, protection, or love. We'll talk more about that in a little bit. But for now, just take notice that when we feel so disconnected from God, we have no one to blame but our sinful selves.

The other relationships that sin quickly ruins are the relationships we have with other people. This category of relationships is even more challenging because it could go wrong in two directions. When it comes to God, he's always there for you, but it might be your own feelings or actions that get in the way. But with other humans it's more complicated. You might do something sinful to someone else, or someone else might do something sinful to you, or you might do sinful things to each other as anger escalates and the relationship crumbles. (Sadly, that happens a lot!) Let's take a moment to think about just a few ways that sin ruins our human relationships.

Selfishness. Whether it's you being selfish and ignoring others or someone doing it to you, nothing ruins a relationship faster than someone saying, "I'm number one!" Sometimes people do this as they hide behind catch phrases like, "I'm just gonna do me right now," or "It's not you, it's me." But you know what they mean. They and their life are more important than you and your life. More often though they don't need to say anything. You can take the hint from their actions.

161

Anger. Let's face it. Without being cliché, we have to admit that we are all sinners. That means we are going to sin against others and others will sin against us. However, when anger defeats Christian love and forgiveness, relationships quickly fall apart. Plain and simple.

Lack of trust. You're only a teen but I bet you've figured this much out by now—trust is tough to earn and even tougher to earn *back*. You've certainly learned that if you've broken the trust of your parents or your friends, or similarly if they've done so to you. At the same time, because this is an imperfect world, sometimes we don't trust people simply because we are suspicious or jealous. There might be no reason for you *not* to trust your boyfriend/girlfriend or your best friend. But then you see that person hanging out all the time with someone else or you see them tagged in tons of pictures with others and you start to become suspicious and your trust wavers.

Laziness. Unfortunately, people who don't love perfectly will therefore not put love and effort into relationships like they should. You kind of just let things go as the status quo and over time your relationship deteriorates. I bet you could think of at least one relationship right now—with a family member, a childhood friend, or a recent friend—where gradually over time you "drifted apart." Yet if you think about it carefully, it's likely that happened because you just didn't put in enough effort.

Preoccupied. This one is a cousin of selfishness and laziness, but slightly different. In this scenario, either you or the other person is likely not trying to ruin your relationship. However, either you or the other person is simply too preoccupied and busy. You've got a million things going on at school, and so does the other person, so the two of you are just too busy to maintain the relationship. Unfortunately the most common place for this to happen is at home. Often it's dad and/or mom who become so preoccupied with "life"—work, bills, errands, etc.—that it is at the expense of their relationship with you. They aren't investing the time, effort, or love that they should.

Self-doubt. I want to make sure that this is mentioned specifically as a problem in relationships. Often times we might be so self-conscious, so shy, so embarrassed, so unsure of ourselves that we may be scared of relationships. That could lead you to shy away from talking to new people, sitting with others in the cafeteria, going to school events, and more. No one did anything to you, but because you have so much self-doubt, you don't engage in any relationships and end up finding yourself feeling very lonely.

There are certainly more things that contribute to the breakdown of relationships, but I'll stop with this shorter list to point something out to you. Did you notice the common thread to all of these things? Can you analyze what sin is behind every one of those problems that occur in relationships? It's pride!

Pride is what leads people to think about themselves before others. Pride is what causes people to dwell on their anger instead of forgiving and loving. Pride is what causes people to think of themselves first and break trust, or else causes them not to trust other people who have earned it. Pride is what makes us more occupied with our own interests so that we are too lazy or too busy to have quality relationships with others. Pride causes impatience, fighting, revenge, and so much more. And whether you are the one caught up in sinful pride, someone else is, or you both are, pride is bound to destroy our relationships.

Have you experienced these things before? Has your own sin interfered with your relationship with God? Have you felt disconnected from him because you feel guilty or embarrassed or simply because you've been spiritually lazy?

How often has sin disrupted your relationships with others? Do you have problems at home because of your attitude toward your parents? Or is your family so busy that you rarely have any time or effort for each other? Maybe it's people at school—how they treat you, what they say to you or about you. Maybe it's your friends. Has your bestie suddenly become your worstie because of something one of you did? Has a dating relationship blown up to pieces because of how you treated each other?

Between God and all the other humans in our lives, there are so many relationships that are so very important to us. But sin interferes quickly! Before we know it, we feel very *dis*connected from God and from others. It makes us want to pull our hair out and exclaim—*I feel so alone!*

When I feel like this, I need something different. I need some facts . . .

Fact: I Am Connected
What a wild night! Talk about an emotional rollercoaster! The closeness of a meal among friends, yet the brokenness of someone about to stab a friend in the back. The warnings about falling away. The talk about him going away. "What? What do you mean you're leaving us?" Their minds must have been a blur and their blood pressures off the charts.

But Jesus knew this. Jesus knew how the disciples were feeling, even though they didn't understand everything yet. Jesus knew what was going to happen in a matter of hours. Jesus knew what the disciples would do and how they would feel even worse after it. Perhaps most of all, Jesus knew that any talk of him suffering, dying, and leaving scared them to death. They didn't want to be alone!

164

Once again, we see Jesus' incredible care and compassion for his disciples on the evening before he died. He had so many other important things to think about, yet he still thought about his disciples. Thus, in the middle of all that was going on, Jesus stopped what he was doing and saying to pray, and he prayed out loud so his disciples then and now could hear. He prayed first for his disciples, then for all believers—including you. This following section of verses is just a little longer, but it is really special. I want you to pay careful attention to the deep love of Jesus pouring out in his words. He wants nothing more than for people to be connected—to him and to each other. Take a look:

> My prayer is not for them alone. I pray also for those who will believe in me through their message, that all of them may be one, Father, just as you are in me and I am in you. May they also be in us so that the world may believe that you have sent me. I have given them the glory that you gave me, that they may be one as we are one—I in them and you in me—so that they also may be brought to complete unity. Then the world will know that you sent me and have loved them even as you have loved me.

> Father, I want those you have given me to be with me where I am, and to see my glory, the glory you have given me because you loved me before the creation of the world.

> Righteous Father, though the world does not know you, I know you, and they know that you have sent me. I have made you known to them, and will continue to make you known in order that the love you have for me may be in them and that I myself may be in them.[147]

Every now and then in the Bible, there are these incredible moments where it's like you can peer right into the heart and

---

[147] John 17:20–26

mind of God. Well if you want to know what God thinks or how he feels about you, look no further. This is it right here— from the mouth of God the Son himself.

Did you hear how Jesus expressed the perfect connection that he has as God the Son with God the Father? Their love for each other is perfect. Their relationship is perfect. Their unity is perfect.

Next, note that there are two things that Jesus specifically prays for. First, Jesus prayed that believers would be one and united with our heavenly Father. Jesus wants nothing more than for us to know and experience the same love, closeness, and unity with the Father that he has. Secondly, Jesus prayed that we would be one with each other. Just as the Father and the Son are united, so Jesus wants so dearly for us to be closely united with each other.

Put on your best geometry thinking cap and picture an equilateral triangle (you know, that thing with three sides of equal length). Imagine God at the top point, you at the right point, and others at the left point. God doesn't want a triangle that has sides miles apart. He wants to shorten the sides. He wants to draw you in closer to himself and to other people, shortening the sides until there is perfect closeness and unity forever in heaven.

Oh, but there's that pesky sin thing, right? You're catching on here, young Jedi Christian! You're right. That sin thing is a HUGE problem. In fact, it is THE problem.

Thankfully Jesus didn't say "Amen" to his prayer and then pack up and go back home to Nazareth. Quite the opposite. As soon as Jesus finished those words you just read, he left and made his way to the Garden of Gethsemane. The time had now arrived. Jesus was about to accomplish for us the very thing that he had just prayed for. He was going to tear down the dividing wall of sin that separates us from God and from each other. He was going to bring unity to us—unity with God and with each other.

And so he went on his way to suffer. He suffered for you and for me. For our pride, for our selfishness, for our anger, for our laziness. For everything. There was hell to pay for how we have ruined relationships with God and with each other by our sins, but Jesus was going to pay it. And he did. After he declared that his work was finished, Jesus cried out in a loud voice, "My God, my God, why have you forsaken me?"[148]

That there is hell. When you think of hell, don't think of some hot place beneath you with some guy in a red jumpsuit with a giant pitchfork. Hell is separation from God *forever*. Hell is when God turns his back on you and takes away his presence, his power, and his love *forever*. Hell is when you are really and truly alone *forever*. And that is what our dear Savior Jesus experienced on the cross. He was abandoned and forsaken by his own heavenly Father to be on his own and alone so that you and I never would have to be. Jesus allowed himself to be *dis*connected from his Father so that we could be *connected* to him. Take a look at how the apostle Paul explains this:

> All this is from God, who reconciled us to himself through Christ and gave us the ministry of reconciliation: that God was reconciling the world to himself in Christ, not counting people's sins against them. And he has committed to us the message of reconciliation.[149]

What sin broke, Jesus fixed. In the Garden of Eden, sin fractured the relationships of humans with God and with each other. But Jesus brought us unity at the cross. He *reconciled* us to God. That's a fancy word that means Jesus restored and repaired the relationship. The dividing wall of sin is gone so that we can be one with God, restored into a loving and special relationship

---

[148] Matthew 27:46
[149] 2 Corinthians 5:18–19

just as Jesus had prayed about the night before. And because we have unity with God, we who believe have unity with each other in that message of reconciliation! Amazing!

This unity that we now have with God is life changing because it completely changes our reality. You might *feel* alone. You might *feel* disconnected from God. But the reality, the truth, the *fact* is that your relationship with God is made perfect in Christ. That leads us to the first fact to consider:

> **Fact #1** – You *are connected.* No matter what you've done or how much you have sinned, Jesus took away your sin and your debt of hell. He tore down the dividing wall of sin and punishment and connected you to God—now and forever.

I'm guessing you've been around the block enough to know though that just because you are connected to someone on paper, that doesn't mean they will be there for you. Too many people have biological parents whom they are connected to by birth, but in reality they are never there for their children. Too many marriages consist of people who are connected on paper but live disconnected lives where neither is present for their spouse. Too many teens post "Happy B-Day to my Day 1 BFF" to look good on someone's story, but never really do anything else for that friend all year long.

Not to worry with God though! Not only are you connected to God through Jesus Christ, but God himself promises that he will be with you. Again, don't take my word for it. Trust the facts of his own words and promises. Listen to these touching words of God through the prophet Isaiah. Like your favorite deliciously soft and chewy cookie, take time to enjoy every morsel of these delightful words:

> Do not fear, for I have redeemed you;
>   I have summoned you by name; you are mine.
> When you pass through the waters,

I will be with you;
and when you pass through the rivers,
    they will not sweep over you.
When you walk through the fire,
    you will not be burned;
    the flames will not set you ablaze.
For I am the LORD your God,
    the Holy One of Israel, your Savior;
I give Egypt for your ransom,
    Cush and Seba in your stead.
Since you are precious and honored in my sight,
    and because I love you,
I will give people in exchange for you,
    nations in exchange for your life.
Do not be afraid, for I am with you.[150]

I'll give you a moment to grab a tissue to dry your eyes. I need to as well. Go ahead and pause to reflect on those words a bit more, and then join me again in the next paragraph.

These words are forever etched into my mind. Not only are the words precious by themselves, but I have one particular day in my mind. I had been working with a teen for hours and hours and hours. We talked almost every day. She had serious depression. She had thought about suicide and was about to do it. She was in my office and in about one hour she was going to leave to spend some time away from all her friends and family to get necessary help at a mental health facility. She was going to be there for an indefinite amount of time, and she was terrified. I read these verses. We prayed together. We cried together. But the Lord held to these promises and was with her through all the deep waters and fiery flames of her troubles. What comfort to know that God loves her so much![151]

---

[150] Isaiah 43:1–5
[151] OK, time out again to wipe away more tears . . .

God loves you so deeply, too. He knows you personally. He cares for you specifically. What can be more touching than to hear God himself say, "I have summoned you by name; you are mine . . . I love you . . . I am with you"? In Christ, God restored his relationship with you. In baptism he called you by name and he put his own name—Father, Son, and Holy Spirit—on you. You belong to him now. So he promises on his end of this relationship that he is with you, he loves you, and you have nothing to fear.

What does that look like? How does that play out in your life? There's hardly a clearer picture and description of how God is with you than in the following beloved words. Buckle up for some more touching words (and maybe some more tissues). Read through this next psalm slowly and cherish every word.

> The LORD is my shepherd, I shall not be in want.
> He makes me lie down in green pastures,
> > he leads me beside quiet waters,
> > he restores my soul.
> He guides me in paths of righteousness
> > for his name's sake.
> Even though I walk
> > through the valley of the shadow of death,
> I will fear no evil,
> > for you are with me;
> your rod and your staff,
> > they comfort me.
> You prepare a table before me
> > in the presence of my enemies.
> You anoint my head with oil;
> > my cup overflows.
> Surely your goodness and love will follow me
> > all the days of my life,
> and I will dwell in the house of the LORD forever.[152]

---

[152] Psalm 23 (NIV 1984 translation)

How often have you felt like you are lost in the valley of the shadow of death? It's like you're a foolish sheep that has strayed from your Good Shepherd and you're disconnected from the flock. You feel lost. You feel surrounded. You feel like danger and disaster are lurking behind every turn or every rock along the winding path of the valley. Have you felt that desperate before? Have you felt that afraid? Have you felt that alone? I know I have.

Listen to the facts though. Not only are you connected with the Lord in this special and loving relationship, but the Lord then in turn promises that he will be there for you. He will provide for your needs like a shepherd who provides grass and water for the sheep. He will lead you on his own righteous path simply because of his own name—the name Yahweh-LORD that reminds us he is faithful to who he is and his promises to us. He will guide you like a shepherd through the darkest valleys with his rod and staff, tools used for both guidance and protection. In fact, you have such peace and calm when your Good Shepherd is with you that it's as if he could spread out a table and you could sit down and have dinner in the midst of all your enemies and never worry once. That's because your Good Shepherd anoints you with oil as his chosen one to the point that blessings overflow like a cup spilling over. Yes, with this Good Shepherd at your side, surely nothing but his good blessings and love will follow you every single day until you dwell with him in heaven forever.

I don't even know how to respond to such wonders of love. I'm speechless. So I'm just going to give you the next fact:

> **Fact #2** – You are connected to God *right now* because *he is with you.* Jesus restored your relationship with God at the cross and now God promises to be with you every step of the way.

Danger! You just heard a fact of God's Word and promises to you. You know what that means. Here come the questions of Satan to plague you with doubt . . .

What if I stray too often?

What if I really messed up?

What if I don't feel like God is with me?

What if God decides to stop being with me?

Even after all that Jesus did with his suffering, death, and resurrection, and even after proving he was alive to his disciples multiple times, they still had their uncertain moments of doubt. They still didn't quite get it (but they would very soon!). Jesus knew this. He always knew what was on their hearts and minds. Thus, as Jesus was about to disappear from their visible sight, he knew that they were afraid. They were afraid about the mission he had just given them to go and make disciples of all nations, and they were afraid that now they would be alone. Jesus knew the perfect words to leave them with: "Surely I am with you always, to the very end of the age."[153]

Don't let the feelings or whispers of doubt creep in for one second. Go back to the facts. Listen to what God himself says. Listen to those words of Jesus. He *is* with you. *Always.* Not some of the time, not only when you act right, not only when life is going well. *All* the time. Jesus is with you *always*.

A number of years after Jesus spoke those words a lot of stuff had gone down. The Christian Church exploded with growth. The good news of Jesus had gone out all over the place. Yet at the same time that the number of believers was increasing, so also was the amount of persecution. The early Christians fought off many troubles—enemies to the faith, false teachings, and all

---

[153] Matthew 28:20

the other sins of the world. They felt at times like they were alone. That's why an unidentified writer sent a letter to the Hebrew people reminding them of how amazing Jesus is.[154] But he also reminded them of a promise that God had made long ago to Moses and the Israelites:

God has said,

> "Never will I leave you;
> never will I forsake you."[155]

ALWAYS and NEVER. These are words that we shouldn't use in our conversations because *always* and *never* are almost always never true. (See what I did there?) You might say you will always do this or that, or never do this or that, but you will eventually fail to keep your word because you're an imperfect sinner. But this is not true with God. He *always* keeps his Word and *never* fails you. (See what I did there again?) And what is his promise to you? He will *always* be with you and *never* leave you or forsake you. This is our third fact:

> **Fact #3** – You are connected to God right now and *he will be with you always.* Jesus was forsaken at the cross so that you never would be. He fixed your relationship with God and guaranteed that the relationship would stand forever. God is with you every step of the way!

One more challenge exists for us to overcome. It's kind of a big one. Alright, so maybe a *really* big one. What about our relationships with other people? Good news! Jesus has taken care of this, too. Just as he fulfilled that beautiful prayer we examined earlier and brought us unity with God, so he also fulfilled that prayer and brought us unity with each other. In

---

[154] Next time you have some free moments for Bible reading, read the book of Hebrews. It is very powerful as it makes clear how superior Jesus is to everyone and everything.

[155] Hebrews 13:5, quoting Deuteronomy 31:6

Jesus there is now a massive community of believers connected to each other and through him.

Actually, if you want to do some smarty-pants Bible reading some time, read the New Testament looking for the sub-theme of unity in Christ. It's all over the place! It starts with the great day of Pentecost. That was the day that the Holy Spirit came to the disciples to empower them to be bold witnesses for Jesus. He also gave them the unique gift of speaking in different languages that they previously didn't know. This was a blessing because there were people from all over the world in Jerusalem at the time. So while there were many languages being spoken at Pentecost, they were really all "talking Jesus" that day. They were united in their Savior.

That theme continues throughout the book of Acts as the early Christians came to realize that Jesus is for everyone—both Jews and Gentiles (non-Jews, or in other words, everyone else). You can read in Galatians how Paul pleads with them to understand that we are all "one in Christ Jesus."[156] Or you can read in Ephesians how he encourages them to "keep the unity of the Spirit"[157] or in 1 Corinthians how he warns against divisions in the church.[158] You can read 1 Thessalonians to see how he carefully encourages them to be and act like a family of believers, "brothers and sisters" in the faith. Or you can see in the opening verses of Philippians how dearly he loved and missed his fellow believers.[159] There are so many more examples. The point is that we have a real unity with one another, and that bond is something special to protect, preserve, and enjoy.

Paul had a special illustration to explain this connection that we have with each other. He explains that our connection is much like the human body.

---

[156] Galatians 3:26–28
[157] Ephesians 4:3
[158] 1 Corinthians 1:10–17
[159] Philippians 1:3–11

Just as a body, though one, has many parts, but all its many parts form one body, so it is with Christ . . . so that there should be no division in the body, but that its parts should have equal concern for each other. If one part suffers, every part suffers with it; if one part is honored, every part rejoices with it.

Now you are the body of Christ, and each one of you is a part of it.[160]

Just as you have one body with many body parts that all work together under the guidance of your head (your brain), so also we are all connected as the body of Christ who is our Head and Leader. There are a number of ways that this is experienced by us in real life. All of them are very special, and I have personally had the privilege of experiencing all of the following:

A global community. I'm not quite sure I have had too many Christian moments in my life that were better than the one I had in a hut. That's right. A hut. My wife and I were with a mission team in the middle of nowhere in Zambia. The congregation's church had burned down and they had a makeshift hut they used as a church. On that day we nine Americans sat on logs and stumps along with African brothers and sisters and expressed unity of faith as we worshiped our one true God and our one Savior Jesus Christ. It was incredible! (I will also add that the singing of their choir was beyond what words could describe! The whole experience was so wonderful!) Do you realize this? Do you realize that you are connected with millions upon millions of Christians around the globe right now? Do you know that if you speak the words of the Nicene Creed or the Apostles' Creed there are millions of Christians who are speaking

---

[160] 1 Corinthians 12:12, 25–27. See also the illustrations in that entire section of verses, as well as the other time he uses this illustration extensively in Romans 12:3–8.

those same words that same day?[161] What a powerful thing to know that you are united with people from all over the planet right now.

A serving community. Going back to that illustration of the body of Christ, think about how your own body works. Each part of your body has a different function. Some parts are more vital than others, but they are all useful and important. When you stub your toe or get poked in the eye or sprain your ankle or wrist, it definitely affects the rest of your body. In the same way, the whole community of believers works together to use their gifts in different ways. Everyone, you included, has different gifts and that's really cool. In my church in Florida, some served on our church council, some were ushers, some handed out service folders, some were on the tech team, some simply made coffee or brought snacks on Sunday morning. So many more served, but all of them collectively were a part of Jesus' awesome work in his kingdom. Look for the gifts of others that you can appreciate and applaud, and then look for ways that you can serve and use your many gifts in the body of Christ!

A fellowshipping community. I snuck in a fancy word there again. *Fellowship* is a word that means to have a *sharing* or *unity* or *community*. It's actually where we get the word *communion* from. So on the one hand, it is a wonderful blessing when we can get together as Christians and eat together as Christians and worship and pray together as Christians. These are examples of Christian fellowship. But the most real expression of unity and oneness and connectedness on earth is actually Holy Communion, or the Lord's Supper. Think about it!

---

161 If you haven't learned or said those ancient creeds of the Christian faith, find them and learn them and say them! They so clearly express our Christian faith as taught in the Bible and they unite us with millions of other Christians who use them! Awesome!

At one and the same time you are both coming together (communing) with Jesus himself who offers to you his body and blood for the forgiveness of your sins,[162] *and* you are coming together (communing) with other believers who are united with you in faith and beliefs. What a powerful thing! If you are feeling *dis*connected from God or from others, I would encourage you to be active in your participation in Holy Communion!

An eternal community. Finally, we remember that the Church of God is more than just the millions here on earth. There are billions of believers already in heaven. You may know some—a family member, a friend, a member of your church. They are there right now enjoying a perfect relationship with God and with each other forever and ever. You are connected with them through faith in Jesus. This is not some fictional, imaginary connection either, as if we just say it to make ourselves feel better when someone dies. Definitely not! Jesus is alive. He is living right now, and as God he is present everywhere—in heaven and on earth. Thus, those living physically on earth and those living eternally in heaven are truly connected by their one living Savior. Talk about hope and comfort!

The Bible is filled with endless encouragement that gives us comforting reminders about life in this world. We are not alone! Yet not only is God with us now and always, but we are also connected to a body of believers that spans both heaven and earth. It's a real, true, close, and loving connection of brothers and sisters in Christ who are children of the same heavenly Father. That brings us to our final fact of the chapter:

> **Fact #4** – You are connected to God through the work of Jesus Christ both now and always. You are also *connected to the entire body of believers* now and always. No

---

[162] See Matthew 26:26–28, 1 Corinthians 10:16, and 1 Corinthians 11:23–29.

matter how you may feel, there are billions of Christians right alongside you as the family of God in Christ Jesus.

Summary

These are crazy times that we live in! In this 21st century we now find ourselves more connected than ever before because of advancements in technology and travel. It is a unique time to be alive when you can connect with people all over the world at any moment.

Yet despite the possibilities, the problems are endless. Technology *dis*connects us as we become attached to our screens. Sin interferes as it disrupts our relationship with God and our relationships with one another. Though we *could* feel very connected to other people, very often we feel just the opposite. At any given time, any one of us might be overwhelmed with loneliness and say—*I feel so alone!* That's when you need to focus on the facts.

Let's review them:

Fact #1 – You are connected to God because of the work of Jesus Christ.

Fact #2 – You are connected to God because of Jesus and God promises to be with you right now.

Fact #3 – You are connected to God because of Jesus both now *and* always.

Fact #4 – You are connected to God and the entire community of believers in heaven and on earth.

What endless blessings! It's all just as God had originally planned! At creation God had designed perfect relationships for humans—both with him and with one another. But sin ruined that. Yet God in his wisdom and grace was able to restore those relationships. This is yours right now in Christ. This is part of your new identity. Just as Jesus is one with the Father and one with us, so are you now one with God and one with fellow believers. It is just as God has planned! And one day soon, those relationships will be confirmed in perfection for all eternity in heaven.

Thus, we return to our glimpses of glory in Revelation. Do you remember the vision we reviewed in the last chapter? John saw the saints and angels praising God and worshiping Jesus, the Lamb. John heard the good news that they are before the throne of God and serve him in endless joy with no pain or sadness or sorrow. But who makes up this group of believers? I'm glad you asked. John tells us a bit earlier in the chapter:

> After this I looked, and there before me was a great multitude that no one could count, from every nation, tribe, people and language, standing before the throne and before the Lamb. They were wearing white robes and were holding palm branches in their hands. And they cried out in a loud voice:
>
> > "Salvation belongs to our God,
> > who sits on the throne,
> > and to the Lamb."[163]

Can you picture it? Can you picture the multitude of believers in heaven? Can you picture a multitude of people that no one can count but God himself? Can you picture this multitude with males and females and black and brown and white people from America and Africa and Australia and everywhere in between and all around? Can you picture yourself there? You will "dwell in the house of the Lord forever" and join in perfect unity with others to sing the praises of our one true God and Savior.

Dear teen, trust the facts. Trust God's words.

You *are* connected!

---

[163] Revelation 7:9–10

179

Chapter 10

Feeling: I Feel Anxious

vs.

Fact: I Am Reassured

Gabriela could feel her heart beating through her chest. Her face was red. Her hands were shaky. Her lungs tightened and she felt like she couldn't breathe. You would think that Gabriela was about to step on stage to sing a solo or take the last second game-winning shot. Nope. She was just sitting on her bed staring at the wall.

It wasn't the first time Gabriela felt like this. There had been so many times, but the first she could remember was around fifth grade. During a busy week of practices and games and homework and the school play, Gabriela was caught by surprise with these strange feelings that froze her like a woolly mammoth in *Ice Age*. Over the years it gradually increased in frequency so that now, as a junior in high school, it seemed to happen nearly every other day. She hated it. The racing heartbeat. The cold sweats. The loss of breath. It was all so overwhelming. But Gabriela couldn't help herself. She worried. A *lot*.

The strange thing is that almost anything could trigger her—big stuff, small stuff, realistic things, unrealistic things—it didn't seem to matter. In middle school she found herself worrying about things like messing up in front of others in the piano recital or forgetting her lines in the school play or that none of her friends would show up at her birthday parties.

Recently though, the worries seemed much more pressing and serious. Freshman year Gabriela had a real rough patch when her dad lost his job. Would he find another one soon? What if he didn't? What if the family lost the house? What if they had to move and she had to find new friends at a new school? What if her friends right now weren't close enough with her to keep in touch if she had to move? What if fights about work and money led to her parents getting divorced?

That was a bad one, but sophomore year was worse. Home life had settled down, but this time the anxious spell was all boy related. Gabriela had started dating a guy she really liked, but no matter how hard she tried, she couldn't keep the worries from flooding into her brain. What if she wasn't pretty enough for him? Why did he talk to Hannah so much? What if they broke up? What if Hannah stole her man? She had spent so much time and effort and gave so much of her heart to this guy, how could she ever move on to someone else? These worries were only made worse by the everyday barrage of worries about school and practices and friends.

Yet none these episodes compared to the epic breakdown Gabriela was now experiencing in her junior year. It's like everything was converging at the same time as the perfect destructive storm. The ACT was only two weeks away and there was no way she was ready for it. What if she got a bad score and had to take it again? What if she took it multiple times and still didn't get the number she wanted? What if the pressure of the ACT got to her and she failed some of the other big tests coming up? What if that caused her to fail those classes? What if one really bad week ruined everything and then she couldn't get into the college she wanted? Then again, that's assuming she could pick a college in the first place. She was almost a senior and still had absolutely no idea what she wanted to do with her life. What if she picked the wrong college? What if she didn't like the career path she chose? What if her parents were disappointed with her choices? What if she picked a bad college and the wrong major and her parents were upset and she didn't talk to her friends anymore and she had to face all these problems by herself? What if . . . ?

Gabriela would have been bawling her eyes out, that is, if she had any more tears left to give. She was pretty cried-out for the week though. She had a breakdown during fourth period on Monday, she freaked out at lunch on Wednesday, she cried all night to her friends on Friday (and she could tell they were annoyed with her and sick of it). Now it was only 10am on Saturday and already her heart was fluttering as her head was flooding with endless thoughts and questions.

Back in grade school Gabriela used to think, "It'll be OK. I'll get through this." In her first years of high school that morphed into, "I better get my act together because this is not normal." Now she didn't know what to think. What if something was wrong with her—like seriously wrong? What if she had to get help? What if her parents would be disappointed in that, too? What if she would be like this forever? What if . . . What if . . . What if . . . ?

Some tears finally started to fall. Unfortunately, she did have more to shed. Well, such is the life of a professional worrier, right? Right??? It seemed like every moment of every day Gabriela was consumed with one overwhelming thought—*I feel so anxious.*

Feeling Anxious

"Anxiety weighs down the heart."[164] How true! There are few things in life that are so all-consuming as anxiety. I'm sure you're all too familiar with that because anxious thoughts can come from anywhere and about anything! I've seen teens have total breakdowns because of friend drama or bad breakups. I've seen

---

[164] Proverbs 12:25

outright panic over grades and test scores. I've witnessed the endless turmoil from endless teens agonizing over college and career choices. I've seen stress over family and student council and prom. I've even coached a quarterback who threw up before every single football game—even as a senior!

Anxiety does a lot to us. It can make us feel unsettled and uneasy. It can make our blood pressure skyrocket or breaths hard to come by. It can cloud our thinking and judgment as if we're living in a foggy haze and can't find our way out of it. It can paralyze us with a fear of making any choices, doing anything, or going anywhere.

Yet at the heart of the matter there seems to be something a bit different—the heart. However, I don't think that Bible verse about anxiety weighing down the heart has anything to do with the critical organ pumping blood throughout your body. Here heart would really mean something like the sum collection of all your thoughts and feelings and emotions. We talk this way often. We say things like, "You stole my heart," or, "My heart goes out to you." In those cases you aren't talking about moving forward in life with a giant hole in your chest. Rather, you mean that your feelings and emotions are with someone else. In the same way, this Bible verse rightly suggests that anxiety can weigh heavily on our emotional, psychological, and even spiritual state (all that "heart" stuff, we might say).

Think about how those things are related. When you are worried and feel anxious, that can lead to a number of different emotions. You might be angry about the situation that worries you. You might be afraid of what could happen. You might be sad about those potentially bad things coming your way. Those emotions can greatly affect us psychologically then. How we start to process life and information and situations and relationships may start to change. Anxiety disorders or various levels of depression may start to grip our minds. All the while, these emotional and psychological struggles may affect our faith as well. We may have spiritual worries or doubts overshadow our trust in God and his Word. Before we know it, our "heart" looks kind of like my extension cord collection—a tangled mess that I might rather throw away than try and figure out because fixing it seems impossible.

TIME OUT!!!

At this point I'm going to take a quick T.O. because we need to have a little talk about anxiety and depression. You will notice in this book that I'm not going to go too technical on you. I'm not throwing all kinds of stats and figures at you, or giving you all kinds of fancy technical and scientific terms and data. Instead, I'm talking about anxiety and worry in a very general way and obviously taking a spiritual approach toward them.

However, let me be very clear: anxiety disorders, depression, and the like are real psychological conditions that ought to be treated seriously and handled with great care. Most of the time it is wise to seek professional help. A school guidance counselor may be good. Seek help there. But a professional, certified Doctor of Psychology would be the most qualified to help you. If you do need help, the best scenario would be for you to *both* see a psychologist *and* talk to your pastor so that they can work hand-in-hand to help your psychological and spiritual state of mind at the same time. It is a very powerful thing to seek help from God's almighty Word *and* to seek help from those God has gifted with knowledge and expertise in the sciences. God gives spiritual and worldly gifts to us to bless us. This is such a case where both can do just that.[165]

Next, we have got to get over this whole, "I'm crazy / you're crazy" thing. It continues to be so disappointing to me to see

---

[165] In full disclosure, my mother is in fact a Doctor of Psychology with her own clinic at this time. I have seen countless occasions where professional counseling has helped immensely. When paired with pastoral counseling, it has indeed been powerful. And yes, sometimes we have actually had the privilege of working to help the same student at the same time—a privilege and a pleasure! ☺

and hear how people talk about professional counseling. Countless teens have been anywhere from afraid to downright refusing because "I'm not crazy. I don't need that." I've also worked with teens that would like to get more help, but they've been deathly afraid of their friends finding out and then saying, "You're crazy!" Or, what really gets me hot is when parents are the culprits. Sadly, I've worked with too many families where the teen most definitely needed some extra help and even wanted it, but the parent(s) refused by saying, "My kid's not crazy. We don't need that."

Let me ask you this: If you had a constant cough that got worse over time to the point of struggling to breathe, would you go to the doctor? Or if you broke a bone in a game, would you go to the doctor? Or if you had any suspicion at all that you might have cancer, you think you might see a doctor like yesterday?

IT IS NO DIFFERENT WITH A PSYCHOLOGIST!

Sometimes there are things that aren't quite right in you. There could be hormonal imbalances. There could be developmental or learning delays you are unaware of. There may be chemical imbalances in your brain. So . . . hmm . . . what do you think you should do? Sit there and try to get better? Or maybe do you think you should see a doctor? I say that with sarcasm, but with a smile and with all love. There is no shame in going to get professional counseling from a psychologist. Instead, be proud that you are brave enough and smart enough to get the right kind of help!

Finally, let's chat about suicide for a moment. I mentioned it very briefly in a footnote earlier in this book. But the topic demands further attention. Suicide is *always* a serious topic. *Always*. There is *never* a time when it is funny or cool or no big deal. *Never*. We are talking about a precious, valuable life here—a life that God gave and that Jesus bought with his precious blood. Those facts alone demand that we treat all life with care and compassion and seriousness.

So first on suicide, I find it absolutely disgusting that over the years teens have come to think it's cool or funny to say, "Go kill yourself." Whether it's a comment in the hallways, or a note passed in class (back when people passed notes), or a comment on social media—every single instance of saying such a thing is sickening. Like I better go get some paper towels to clean up my keyboard cuz I'm gonna hurl kind of sickening. This is sin. Period. This is something that you *never* say to someone *ever*, even if you're joking. It's not funny because quite frankly, far too many teens have listened and followed instructions. If you've never said this or typed this, great. Never do it. If you have, I suggest you take a brief moment to repent, rejoice that Jesus has washed you clean, and then find a time in love to apologize to that person.

Next on suicide, if you know someone that is struggling with suicidal thoughts, *always* get help. *Always*. It's not your job to be a professional counselor. It's not your job to fix the situation. It's not even your job to determine whether they really meant it or not. If you know someone who has talked about suicide, thought about it, or even started the planning stages, take it to an adult every time. I'm sorry, but you as a teen are not equipped to handle that situation, nor do you understand all the things that might be going on for that person psychologically. Quite frankly, it's tough on most adults, but at least they know of some things that can be done. A teacher, guidance counselor, school administrator, a pastor, or even a parent are all good choices for people to tell. It is far better to be safe and to protect the person. Loving your friends and classmates is not protecting their secret suicidal thoughts. Loving them is protecting their life and getting them help. *Always*.

Lastly, if you have had (or now have) suicidal thoughts, please, my dear teen, please, go get help. I just gave you a list. Start somewhere—a pastor, a teacher, a guidance counselor, a school administrator. Yes, even your parents. They need to know, too. They want to know. Yes, I know it's scary. It's scary to admit if you're having those thoughts. It's scary to let people know that you're struggling or scary to think that you might let someone down. But my dear teen, I beg you to know and to trust that the adults in your life love you way too much for that. They simply want to see you healthy and happy—emotionally, psychologically, and spiritually. And if none of those options work, email me and I'll help find you the proper help.[166] You are far too valuable to our God for your life not to be protected. So please, get help!

Serious talk about anxiety, depression, and suicide over.

TIME IN!

Back to our general talks about anxiety and worry in our lives. It seems to me that there are several main areas of anxiety that cause us to worry in our lives. Again, this is not a scientific list from a textbook. Rather, these are common areas that seem to cause us the most stress, anxiety, and worry. Let's think about some of them.

> General anxieties. Sometimes you can't put your finger on it because any random thing could cause you to worry and feel anxious. Maybe one time it's the stress of a busy week of school with tests and assignments. Maybe another time it's a new job or a new boss that make you worry. Or it could be just another random, regular day and that makes you anxious because who knows what awful thing might be lurking ahead on a normal day. Sometimes the common things of life can cause you to be very anxious.

> Social anxieties. Other times people worry about very specific things. One common source of worry is other people. Maybe you don't like hanging around big groups of people because you worry what they might think about you or that you won't fit in or that it won't be

---

[166] phil.huebner17@gmail.com

your vibe. It could be that your friends stress you out. All the drama, all the backstabbing, all the gossip—it all makes you anxious about what problem might be next. Of course social media brings plenty of anxiety as well with the constant comparing, verbal fighting, and time spent on creating the perfect persona and profile for the online world to see. Talk about stress! [167]

Family anxieties. To be even more specific, unfortunately for some it is their family that brings extra levels of anxiety. Parents constantly put on the pressure for perfection with unrealistic demands for achievement. They're all over your case about college or career choices. They're all up in your business and don't give you any personal space. They fight with you simply because they're fighting with each other. Sometimes parents are so out of touch with reality that they make the big mistake of saying, "Well in my day . . ." Talk about stress!

Potential trauma anxieties. I like to call this Worst-Case Scenario-ism. Have you ever found yourself caught in this thinking? It goes something like this: What if I fail this test? If I fail this test, I might not pass the class, and if I don't pass the class that will go on my transcripts. If that becomes official, then I won't get into the college of my dreams. What if I don't get into the college of my dreams and then I get a terrible job and I don't like it and I can't provide for my family and life is just awful?! Worst Case Scenario-ism sneaks up on you all the time, from assuming that your boyfriend/girlfriend who isn't responding to a text is out with someone else to worrying that your parent who is two hours late got in an accident and died. Our minds love to fill us with anxiety as we worry about the worst possible scenario happening

---

[167] FYI, Generalized Anxiety Disorder and Social Anxiety Disorder are examples of real conditions that a psychologist might diagnose.

to us—when likely nothing even close to that has taken place yet!

Future anxieties. Finally, we should specifically mention worrying about the future. In my experience, I don't see this really become too serious until late in the sophomore year of high school. Then it can start to get really bad into the junior and senior year. Future anxieties come from all the big life questions going through a teen's mind as they stare their future in the face. What college should I choose? Or should I go military or trade? What career do I want to pursue? What if I make the wrong choice? How am I going to take care of myself now? What happens when I step out of my little bubble? All of these future worries can cause extreme anxiety for teens as they step toward their future and "adulting."

Satan loves all this! He loves to plant questions, doubts, and worries in our minds so that we question God and maybe—just maybe—might turn away from him. Remember that his goal is not just that you sin, but that you are separated from God eternally. Thus, worry is a big deal because it can lead to severe faith problems!

Have you had problems with some of the things we've been talking about? Do you find yourself worrying? A little bit? Some of the time? All the time? Do you ever find that your worries overwhelm you and control you? This can happen very quickly, and suddenly it feels like nothing in life is right or will ever be right. Perhaps at times you might want to shout out in stress—*I feel so anxious!*

When I feel like this, I need something different. I need some facts . . .

Fact: I Am Reassured

Talk about social anxiety! Can you imagine being jam-packed with thousands of other people, all clamoring to see, to touch, or to hear one person? But this wasn't a Post Malone or Beyoncé concert. The situation was much more serious. The crowds had so much more on their minds: My mother is sick and might die . . . I'm not sure we will be able to put food on the table . . . The government is too oppressive . . . My family might fall apart.

Thousands gathered to one place. Thousands filled with worry and anxiety. Thousands hoping that this one person, Jesus, might somehow fix it all.

You or I might be overwhelmed with anxiety just thinking about such a crowd, a crowd mostly confused about who the Messiah was and what he was going to do. Not Jesus though. He saw the opportunity to teach. That was the context when Jesus preached his famous Sermon on the Mount, and in the middle of that sermon he offered the most comforting words. We've already looked at these words once before in Chapter 7, but they are so beautiful that we need to explore them again. Plus, we need to add a few verses and look at these words from a different angle this time. Take your time to fully digest these wonderful words:

> Therefore I tell you, do not worry about your life, what you will eat or drink; or about your body, what you will wear. Is not life more than food, and the body more than clothes? Look at the birds of the air; they do not sow or reap or store away in barns, and yet your heavenly Father feeds them. Are you not much more valuable than they? Can any one of you by worrying add a single hour to your life?

> And why do you worry about clothes? See how the flowers of the field grow. They do not labor or spin. Yet I tell you that not even Solomon in all his splendor was dressed like one of these. If that is how God clothes the grass of the field, which is here today and tomorrow is

191

thrown into the fire, will he not much more clothe you—you of little faith? So do not worry, saying, "What shall we eat?" or "What shall we drink?" or "What shall we wear?" For the pagans run after all these things, and your heavenly Father knows that you need them. But seek first his kingdom and his righteousness, and all these things will be given to you as well. Therefore do not worry about tomorrow, for tomorrow will worry about itself. Each day has enough trouble of its own.[168]

Did you soak up every word? There's a lot to chew on and digest here! Last time we explored these words we pondered the care that God has for each person. If he cares for birds and flowers, wouldn't he care for you? Now we can expand that thought. If your heavenly Father cares for you, why would you worry?

Jesus gives some practical examples using necessities of life—clothing, food, and drink. We need those things, so if we are in danger of not having them, it might be a great cause for worry. Jesus' point though is that if God would clothe flowers with beauty and splendor and feed seemingly insignificant birds, won't he also provide for you?

There are two verses here that always catch me and stop me dead in my tracks. The first one is this: "Can any one of you by worrying add a single hour to your life?" Ouch! That one hurts. I worry so much about so many things, but what does that ever accomplish? Think about it. How many times have you experienced a really tough time and then later thought to yourself, "You know what? I really worried my way out of that one! I didn't think I was going to make it through, but sure enough, I just worried and worried and worried some more and that fixed it all! Who knew? All I needed to do was worry enough and that would make everything better!" That's more ridiculous than an episode of the Kardashians show. Jesus

---

[168] Matthew 6:25–34

exposes me every time there, and I'm guessing the same is true for you. What does worrying actually contribute to our lives?

The other verse that takes my breath away is this one: "For the pagans run after all these things, and your heavenly Father knows that you need them." It's the kind of verse that makes me think, "What in the world am I doing here? Why am I worrying so much?! I should know better!" Of course we need things like clothing and food and drink, and yes you need to decide what you're going to do with your life someday, and yes I have concerns about providing for my family. But unbelievers are the ones who chase after these things with frantic worry. We, however, have a heavenly Father who *knows what we need*. He knows what your concerns are. He knows what you need. He knows what you want. He'll take care of it!

Thus, Jesus refocuses us with these key words: "But seek first his kingdom and his righteousness, and all these things will be given to you as well." Our greatest concern can be our relationship with God and our pursuit of his kingdom and his righteousness as we connect with him through his Word and Sacraments. When we pursue the First things first, all these other things—all these other worries of life—will be taken care of too.

OK, I hear you, Jesus. Those are amazing, comforting words. But what if—here comes that dumb devil stuff again—what if God doesn't listen? What if it's too small for God? What if God doesn't care? What if it still doesn't work out?

Oh, that devil and oh those feelings of anxiety! Not to worry though. I'm glad you asked those questions because there are some important facts to share with you . . .

We could imagine that Jesus' disciples were filled with worries as his death was approaching. Jesus knew that and had touching words of comfort for them.[169] Listen to the words Jesus spoke to hearts overwhelmed with worry and anxiety:

> Do not let your hearts be troubled. You believe in God; believe also in me. My Father's house has many rooms; if that were not so, would I have told you that I am going there to prepare a place for you? And if I go and prepare a place for you, I will come back and take you to be with me that you also may be where I am. You know the way to the place where I am going.[170]

Satan wants you to worry by plaguing you with this question: Why shouldn't I worry? Jesus gives us the answer. "ME," he says. We don't need to let our hearts be troubled because we trust in Jesus. Then Jesus gives us some reasons in these verses why we can trust him:

1) God has plenty of space for us in heaven. It's the dopest crib you could ever imagine, and there's a room reserved for *you*! Jesus says that if that wasn't the case, he wouldn't have told us about it in the first place!

2) If Jesus goes to prepare a place for us there (which he did), then he promises that he will come back to take us there (which he will). That's his guarantee to us.

3) This isn't like *Pirates of the Caribbean*. We don't need some complicated map to find this treasure. It's simple. We know the way to be there in heaven where there are no worries or concerns.

---

[169] Are you catching on yet that I keep turning to Holy Week and Jesus' suffering, death, and resurrection? Not only is that the height of Jesus' love and work for us, but it still boggles my mind that, in the midst of all that was going on, Jesus cared enough to take time for his disciples and offer them (and us) the most precious and comforting words!

[170] John 14:1–4

We're a little slow though sometimes, and our puny human brains struggle to process these comforting truths. The same was true for the disciples. Thomas said this: "Lord, we don't know where you are going, so how can we know the way?"[171] Yikes, bro. Really? Yes, really, and I know that I'm that clueless sometimes, too. That's what fear, doubt, worry, and anxiety can do to us! So for all of us who have minds clouded by sin and worry just like Thomas, Jesus made it absolutely clear. "Jesus answered, 'I am the way and the truth and the life.'"[172]

Do you want to know the way to heaven where there will be no problems to worry about and where anxiety will never fill your heart and mind again? It's Jesus.

Do you want to know the truth about a life of peace and joy filled with the love of God found in his forgiveness and waiting for you in heaven? It's Jesus.

Do you want to know about a life that is in a close relationship with God that is free from the burden of sin and that points toward a perfect life in heaven? It's Jesus.

Yet once again, Jesus didn't just speak words of comfort, he carried them out and proved them.

Shortly after he spoke those words, Jesus would find himself in an overwhelming moment. As true God he knew what was coming in the next few hours and as true man he knew how awful it would be. He told his disciples, "My soul is overwhelmed with sorrow to the point of death."[173] But instead of worrying or doubting his heavenly Father, he prayed fervently concluding with these powerful words: "Yet not as I will, but as you will."[174] Jesus maintained perfect trust in his heavenly Father even in moments that were overwhelming.

---

171 John 14:5
172 John 14:6
173 Matthew 26:38
174 Matthew 26:39

Need more proof? Fast forward a few hours to see the Savior hanging from a cross. There he would carry all our doubts, all our questions, all our needless worries and anxieties that come from hearts that don't trust him perfectly. Those too would be paid for. Those too would be washed away and erased. Those too would be forgiven.

Need more proof yet? Fast forward to that first Easter morning and see the empty tomb. Our worries about our spiritual or eternal well-being are crushed under the feet of the Savior who conquered Satan, death, and hell.

You see, the point is that when Jesus says to us, "Do not let your hearts be troubled . . . believe also in me," he then gives us every reason to put our trust in him as we put our worries away and to rest. When God speaks, he always says what he means and means what says, and then does what he says, too. This leads us to our first fact to consider:

> **Fact #1** – You are *reassured*. You are reassured by Jesus himself that you don't need to worry. You can put your faith and trust in him. And Jesus is trustworthy—he has proven this by his life, death, and resurrection for you!

So Jesus is trustworthy. Point made. Fact proven. Who can argue with his track record as God? Who can argue with what he has done? He is clearly an almighty Savior-God that is worthy of being trusted. But anxious hearts may wonder and start to worry, "How do I know this almighty God of the universe really cares about me? How do I know he'll help little old me with my puny problems? Doesn't he have more important things to take care of?"

If that's what you think, not to worry! (No, seriously. Don't worry!) There is a Bible verse just for you to address those thoughts. Here are the encouraging words of Peter: "Cast all your anxiety on him because he cares for you."[175] Now that is one special verse! Let's dissect it a bit, shall we?

Pop quiz! What part of speech is that first word in the sentence, the verb (Cast)? Well if you forgot some of your basic English lessons, don't worry. (See again! Don't worry!) *Cast* is an imperative, or a command. That's pretty awesome actually. God doesn't say, "Hey, if you feel like it, or get around to it, or if it ever comes to mind, shoot me a text and let's see what happens." No, this is a command from God. He is telling you, "Do it! Cast it! Throw it!"

Alright, so cast what, Lord? The answer is right there plain as day. God is commanding you to cast *your anxiety*. Heap it up and throw it!

WAIT! Wait a minute! Like what kind of anxiety are we talking about? The big stuff only? The epic life-shaking moments? The stuff that really gets us worked up? NO! Not at all! God says to cast *all* your anxiety.

But where? Where should I put this anxiety? Should I suck it up, buttercup? Should I figure it out somehow? Should I go to a self-help book? NO! God says to cast all your anxiety *on him*.

Now hold on here. That's nice of God, but why should I do that? Why would a holy and perfect God in his holy heaven listen to the anxieties of a poor and pathetic sinner like me? Are you ready for the awesome part? Take a deep breath. Here it is: *because he cares for you.* That's right. Little old you with your little old problems are in no way little or insignificant to God. He has proven this to you in Jesus. God so loved the world that he sent his Son, and you're in "the world," my friend. You *are* loved by God (Chapter 5) and you *are* priceless to God (Chapter 7). So now be reassured with this second fact:

---

[175] 1 Peter 5:7

Fact #2 – You are reassured that God *cares for you*. Jesus himself tells you that you need not worry. You can trust in who Jesus is and what he says, and thus you can trust your Savior God when he says he cares specifically for you.

That devil is relentless though! We've looked at two wonderful facts of Scripture that reassure us of God's love and that he cares for us specifically and individually. But that won't stop Satan from attacking. Even though you hear the words that God cares for you, Satan is going to plant these thoughts in your mind:

I'll believe it when I see it!

Show me the proof!

How can God care for me if this bad thing is happening?

This is where some spiritual perspective is needed in our lives. This is where spiritual maturity is of greatest value. And I always promise to keep it 100 with you, so I have to say at this point, sorry, but you aren't very good at this, my dear teens. Not yet. Sorry, but teens rarely have enough life experience and maturity to have this kind of spiritual perspective. Then again, I'll also be honest and say that adults struggle with this too!

Many times we live our lives like horses with blinders on, meaning that we are only focusing on what is right in front of our face. For example, a teen gets a devastating grade in a class and goes on a 10 minute rant, "I'm gonna die. This is the end of me. My life is over. My future is gone." Or a teen gets dumped and declares, "O-M-Goodness! I can't live without him! I'll never love anyone ever again!" You get the picture, right?

The point is that we all do this kind of stuff, and the more severe the situation the more we obsess over it. Severe sicknesses, cancer, family tragedies, deaths of loved ones—these are all things that seem like insurmountable suffering. (Need I also mention that they bring anxiety and worry?!) These things all make us wonder, "Wait! Does God really care for me?"

There are many verses that could be shared here, but I'm going to turn to one of the more famous ones that is so clear and so comforting. Look at these amazing words of the apostle Paul:

> And we know that in all things God works for the good of those who love him, who have been called according to his purpose. For those God foreknew he also predestined to be conformed to the image of his Son, that he might be the firstborn among many brothers and sisters. And those he predestined, he also called; those he called, he also justified; those he justified, he also glorified.[176]

Look at the confidence Paul starts with—we *know*. We *know* that in all things God works for our good. Not a few things. Not most things. *All* things. We know that God works for our good in all things.

Well if Paul is talking with that kind of confidence, then he must have some facts to go on, right? Right! Remember, we focus on facts and not feelings around here! The facts Paul presents are in the verses that follow. First of all, we have this incredible fact of knowing that God *foreknew* us. This means that God personally knew each and every one of us in advance, even before the creation of the world.

Next, God also *predestined* us. That's a fancy word that has caused a lot of people problems over the years, but I'll break it down simply. The word picture behind it is to "set a fence around." Think of a fence around cattle on a ranch. So when God predestined you, it's like he put a fence around you and said, "You are mine! You belong to me! You are my child!" even

---

[176] Romans 8:28–30

before you were born. That might hurt our brains to think about, but considering that God can look backwards and forwards in time simultaneously with no problems, then we might begin to understand it's no biggie for God to know at the beginning of the story that you will be his child at the end of the story.

Finally, we see the purpose of this work of God. WARNING! RED ALERT! THE POINT OF THE BOOK IS COMING UP HERE . . . Paul wrote that God foreknew and predestined us, "to be conformed to the image of his Son." Yup. You got it. There's your "identity in Christ" verse. God's plan is that he would bring you into his family as his child and that through Jesus you would be his dearly loved child that would live with him in perfection and glory in heaven forever, just like Christ. That's why he goes on to say that Jesus would be the firstborn— he would be God's firstborn Son and would accomplish all this—and many brothers and sisters would follow (that's us).

Therefore, since we *know* that God has done all this in love for us, then we can also *know* that God works all things for our good. Again, not just some things or most things. All things. God works every last thing in your life for your good. To help you understand that, Paul walks you through a little life timeline to help you understand God's ongoing work in eternity just for you and for me. Take a look at the steps he presents in the last verse:

Step 1: Predestined
Even before the creation of the world God knew you and knew that you would be his.

Step 2: Called
Once you were physically alive in this world, God called you to faith. He came to you and actively worked in your life and brought you to faith by his Word.

200

Step 3: Justified
When you came to faith in Jesus Christ, his work of justification[177] became yours personally so that you are now forgiven and innocent in God's sight.

Step 4: Glorified
As a forgiven and now-righteous person in God's sight, the glory of Christ belongs to you right now. And even better, one day soon you will bask in that glory forever in heaven.

Take a step back for a moment and look at that timeline. It spans from one end of eternity to the other—from before creation to you being in heaven forever. God is telling you that every last thing that happens on the timeline he is working for your good and for mine as he is leading us toward the glory of heaven. Think about when you live in history and where you live in the world and the people that God has put in your life. All of this has been part of a master plan *for you*, so that God could bring you into his family with a new identity in Jesus, and then lead you on toward the glory of heaven.

Now look more closely at your life. All those great moments and not so great moments, the highs and the lows, the everything—it's all part of what God is using to work for your good. Maybe struggles are a reminder that God is most important. Maybe sickness is strengthening your trust in him over time. Maybe a bad breakup is leading you to the future love of your life and a wonderful Christian spouse who will help you stay in the faith until death. We don't know *how* God is doing it, but we do know *what* he is doing—he's working everything for our good. That's our next fact:

Fact #3 – You are reassured by God that he works for your good. You can trust who Jesus is and that he cares

---

[177] Remember this is that fancy word we've talked about that means "to declare not guilty."

for you personally, and you can also trust that he works personally for you and for your good in *all* things.

But don't sit there and wonder if God is like the guy that chucks a bucket of paint at a canvas, lets it slide and spill chaotically, and then says, "Look! I've created a masterpiece!" God is far too wise to let things run amok in chaos. As God works for our good in all things, he is much more precise. Take a look at this verse:

> "For I know the plans I have for you," declares the LORD, "plans to prosper you and not to harm you, plans to give you hope and a future."[178]

In recent times, this is one of the most popular and frequently quoted Bible verses in American culture. You can find it everywhere—Christian artwork, jewelry, window clings, tattoos, and more. BIG problem though. Like *really* big. This is probably one of the most *mis*understood verses in the Bible.

The vast majority of people who quote this Bible verse have a wrong understanding of it. Everyone gets the "I have plans for you" part. But it's the next part where people go astray—the part about "plans to prosper you and not to harm you." Many people think that this is God's promise to make earthly life great, such as these examples:

> I just lost my job, but not to worry! God will prosper me! I'll get a better job and make more money in no time!

> My girlfriend just broke up with me, but that's OK! God promises to give me a future, so I know the love of my life is right around the corner and soon I'll be married with three beautiful children!

---

[178] Jeremiah 29:11

Mom just got diagnosed with cancer, but God promises not to harm us, so I know she'll be healed soon!

Now some of those things might happen, but they also might not. While it is true that God promises to bless and keep us in this earthly life, it is *not* true that God promises to give us every earthly thing we ever wanted or dreamed of. At the same time, it is *not* true that God promises your life will be magical cupcakes and unicorns. Quite the opposite. Jesus told us that life in a sinful world among sinful people will be quite difficult!

What we need then is the proper perspective on this verse. The key to understanding it lies in the last phrase. God wants to give you "hope and a future." He's not talking about millions, mansions, and a Maserati though. He's talking about heaven. He's talking about eternal life. He's talking about the riches of his kingdom being yours now and into eternity.

Thus, this verse ties in nicely with the Romans verses we just explored. When God says he works all things for your good, he means it. When God says he has plans for you, he does. But understand that God's plans in working for your good are his plans to bring you into his kingdom now and forever.

One last illustration to help: A little girl went to an art museum with her family one day. She meandered through the rooms of the museum, browsing at various paintings. At one point she turned into a room and found herself staring at a ginormous painting that stretched from floor to ceiling. "Daddy, I don't get it!" she said. "What is it?" Her dad smiled and said, "Come back here, honey." The little girl went to the back of the room and turned around to look at the painting. "Ooooh! I see! I get it now!" she exclaimed as she stared at the most beautiful sunset over the ocean. You see, she couldn't tell what was going on when she was up close and staring at the individual brushstrokes, but when she saw the big picture, she finally saw a masterpiece.

In the same way, so often we get caught up in the individual brushstrokes of our lives, "This seems really bad! This seems out of place! This doesn't make sense!" Meanwhile, God the Master Painter is working out a masterpiece that is taking us from one side of eternity to the other. One day soon enough you will be in heaven and you will say, "Ooooh! I see! I get it now!" That leads us to our final fact of this chapter:

> **Fact #4 –** You are reassured by God that he has specific plans for you. You can trust in Jesus and you can trust that he specifically cares about you. Because he does, he works all things in your life for your good and according to his plans, which ultimately are *plans to bring you to heaven.*

Summary

There are endless things in our lives that lead us to worry. Family, friends, relationships, school, homework, work, our futures—these are just some of the things that weigh heavily on our minds. Sometimes we become so worked up that it's like a hurricane of emotions is ripping through our hearts and minds. All the "things" of life grip us with worries that make us want to cry out—*I feel so anxious!* That's when you need to focus on the facts.

Let's review them:

> Fact #1 – You are reassured about Jesus by who he is and what he has done. He is worthy of your trust at all times.

> Fact #2 – You are reassured that God cares for you personally and specifically.

> Fact #3 – You are reassured that God cares for you by working all things for your good.

Fact #4 – You are reassured that God works all things for your good with specific plans for you that will lead you on to the hope and future of life in heaven.

I will confess that I struggled a bit with what word to choose for the fact of this chapter. There is really not a good opposite word to "anxious," and a lot of words would be great facts that help with anxiety—God's peace, God's plans, God's care, among others. But I chose *reassured* because I want you to understand something very clearly. When things seem iffy and doubts and worries creep in, God not only assures you that he loves and cares for you, but he also *re*assures you—over and over and over again. Thus, as a child of God you can have all the confidence in the world that there is no need to worry about tomorrow. Just as Jesus had perfect trust in his heavenly Father's plans, so can you. That is your identity in Christ. You too are a child of the heavenly Father and a part of his perfect plans! And those plans lead to heaven!

We return then to our sneak peek of the glory that is ours there in heaven as John saw and recorded it in Revelation. We discussed in this chapter that God's plans for you have been in place from one end of eternity to the other. Well, take a look at what the end of your plan looks like. Try to soak in and enjoy every word and picture here:

> Then I saw "a new heaven and a new earth," for the first heaven and the first earth had passed away, and there was no longer any sea. I saw the Holy City, the new Jerusalem, coming down out of heaven from God, prepared as a bride beautifully dressed for her husband. And I heard a loud voice from the throne saying, "Look! God's dwelling place is now among the people, and he will dwell with them. They will be his people, and God himself will be with them and be their God. 'He will wipe away every tear from their eyes. There will be no more death' or mourning or crying or pain, for the old order of things has passed away."

He who was seated on the throne said, "I am making everything new!" Then he said, "Write this down, for these words are trustworthy and true."

He said to me: "It is done. I am the Alpha and the Omega, the Beginning and the End. To the thirsty I will give water without cost from the spring of the water of life. Those who are victorious will inherit all this, and I will be their God and they will be my children."[179]

What a day this will be! All the worries and anxieties of life will be done away with because God will renew everything for us. We will be dressed gloriously as the bride of Christ and all tears will be wiped away, and all death, mourning, and pain will be gone forever.

The almighty God, Jesus the Alpha and Omega, declares to you "It is done." Be reassured that in his book, these plans for you are as good as done. The victory is yours. The new life is yours. The glory is yours. It's all yours in Jesus.

Dear teen, trust the facts. Trust God's words.

You *are* reassured!

---

179 Revelation 21:1–7

Chapter 11

Feeling: I Feel Afraid

vs.

Fact: I Am at Peace

The envelopes had been sitting on the desk in a shoebox for months. The messy pile was almost symbolic of the chaotic mess going on in Ty's head. On the one hand, Ty knew that his future was right around the corner. Unlimited possibilities were potentially hidden inside those envelopes. On the other hand, unlimited problems and challenges awaited as well. He knew he had to open those college letters at some point. His mother nagged him nearly every day about it. But for some reason he just couldn't bring himself to look at them, let alone even think about his future.

Ty had been like this for a while though. His first day of high school was a train wreck. No one would have known it, but to him it was. That morning he nearly faked sick to get out of going to school. He had to pep-talk himself in one of the bathroom stalls to get his act together and get to class. He forced himself to sit with people he didn't know in the cafeteria (and he hated every minute of it). He was sure that at least three seniors laughed at him as he failed to open up his locker. He felt like an idiot in no less than four of his classes. The day was actually quite the normal freshman day, but on the inside Ty was terrified of this big new school.

Eventually Ty overcame those fears and school became mostly tolerable. He made a couple friends and that made it much better. The next big issue was right around the corner though—the school play. In kindergarten he killed it as "Tree #2" and all the parents thought he was hilarious. But that was a long time ago, and this was a much bigger deal. The thought of making new friends and owning the stage and entertaining thousands over a weekend seemed really cool, yet there was so much that could go wrong! What if the director didn't like him? What if he couldn't learn his lines? Even worse, what if he froze during a performance and the entire show bombed because of him? As you might guess, Ty never auditioned. He couldn't bring himself to find the courage.

This sort of seemed to be the theme of his life. He didn't pursue girls much. What if they thought he was weird? What if they told their friends he was weird? What if all the girls in his class talked about how weird he was on Snapchat? He didn't want to be the meme of the century! Better safe than sorry!

Go right down the list: Student Council? Nope. Why would anyone care about his ideas for change? Sports? No way. Who would like him if he messed up a game or brought the team down? Try out for the play sophomore or junior year? Never! Fighting his stage fears that one time freshman year was more than enough.

For all these fears, there was definitely one that trumped them all though. Ty was terrified to let people know who he really was. What if they found out? What would they say? What would they do to him? What if they knew he was a Christian?

Ty's school was a *big* public high school and there were plenty of voices speaking out against Christianity. A number of teachers talked about how silly it was to believe in God as they talked about evolution. Countless classmates talked about how stupid it was to go to church or believe in some "make believe God." Most of the kids in the school bragged non-stop on social media about how high or drunk they were each weekend or how many people they slept with each month.

Ty used to be that kid back in the day in the Sunday School Christmas service who would belt out the Bible recitations and the Christmas songs with his church friends. He loved going to youth group activities. He enjoyed going to church regularly with his family. Most would consider him a strong Christian.

High school was a different animal though. The frequent slams against Christianity, the non-stop barrage of temptations, the constant feeling that he had to defend himself—it was all a bit too much. Ty was so confident in Jesus as his Savior, yet at the same time he was frightened by the thought of letting anyone know.

After all these experiences, now that pile of envelopes was staring at him. What would college bring? How would he make new friends? How much worse would the temptations be? How intense would the pressure and persecution be? And how could he deal with all of that while at the same time walking into a future filled with endless unknowns?

Ty always seemed to have the feeling, but now he could finally identify it. Part of him didn't want to admit it, and part of him wanted to shout it from the rooftops to get it all out. Ty couldn't stop obsessing about one thing—*I feel so afraid.*

Feeling Afraid

Have you noticed something yet? Have you noticed that for all the feelings we have explored, you could say that fear is likely behind all of them? Think about that for a second:

> I feel unloved. The fear is that the most basic need for humans—to be loved and to share love—is something that you can't or won't experience. Moreover, the fear is that because of your sin God doesn't love you either.

209

I feel guilty. The fear is that your sins will not only cause God not to love you, but they will be held against you and you will be separated from God now and forever.

I feel worthless. The fear is that you are a nobody, a nothing that no one cares about or that possibly God doesn't even care about.

I feel weak. The fear is that you can't handle or make it through any situation that comes your way, whether that's an earthly struggle or a spiritual struggle.

I feel alone. The fear is that as you go through life no one will love you, help you, support you, or encourage you, including God.

I feel anxious. The fear is that nothing will work out for good and that everything will fall apart because nothing seems to be in your control or God's control.

Fear drives us to so many different emotions, and fear can often drive us to do so many different things. Sometimes crazy things.

In 2001, there was a TV show that debuted and aired for about five years called *Fear Factor*. If you're bored and like to be freaked out, you can still catch it on Hulu or Netflix. On this show contestants would have three major fear challenges to overcome. If you could overcome all three, you could win $50,000. Common challenges included crazy things like being buried alive for a certain amount of time, insane activities at insane heights, and everyone's favorite, being covered in terrifying creatures like spiders, scorpions, or snakes. In some challenges, contestants would back out in a matter of seconds because they were so terrified. Other times they would start a challenge and completely freeze, paralyzed by fear. Even though they knew when the challenges would be over or that they were secured by safety harnesses, sometimes they would quit just seconds or inches away from $50,000. Fear will do crazy things to you!

Now think about how fear drives behavior in your life. Fear of failing in class leads people to cheat. Fear of an unfaithful boyfriend/girlfriend leads to suspicion, doubt, or social media stalking. Fear of being rejected leads people to act out to try and get noticed or get attention. Fear of death leads to trillions of dollars spent on countless pills, products, and procedures. The list can go on and on.

You probably know you can go online and google different phobias and find all kinds of strange fears. I am a much better writer though than to be so cliché as to throw out random fears like nomophobia, ablutophobia, or phobophobia and make you look them up. I would never do such a thing.[180] But from all the strange fears to all the common fears like the fear of death or public speaking, I'm going to suggest to you that there is really only one fear that every person has—the fear of the unknown. (By the way, I would also never want to put into your head a song you can't get rid of about going "into the unknown" from *Frozen 2*.)[181]

Hear me out on this "fear of the unknown" though. Let's say you are afraid of heights. You might be terrified in the moment that you are on a ladder or on the lookout deck of the Empire State Building overlooking all of New York City.[182] But what are you really afraid of? Aren't you afraid of possibly falling and possibly dying?

You might be afraid of taking the ACT, but what are you really afraid of? Aren't you afraid of the results and how that might affect your future, or at least how your parents or others will think about you and your score?

---

[180] See what I did there?
[181] See what I did there again?
[182] Definite bucket list if you haven't done it. It's incredible!

You might be afraid of something you have done in the past, maybe a bad or secret sin you have committed. But aren't you really afraid of someone finding out, or that sin coming back to haunt you, or getting in trouble, or even how God will treat you?

Let's say you are diagnosed with cancer. That is certainly scary, yet aren't you really afraid of the pain you will experience and the possibility of death?

Or let's talk about death itself. There's a myriad of fears that come with the thought of death. How will you die? What will happen to your loved ones? Where will you be? Is everything you believed about God really true? Will you be in heaven? Would you be in heaven right away or sometime in the future?

As humans, we know absolutely nothing more than what is happening in the exact present moment of right now. As I lazily recline in my bed typing right now, for all I know a meteor might fall in my backyard outside my window in the next ten minutes. Or maybe a scary clown will pop out from under my bed. (Talk about fear!) Everything else in life besides this present moment, even just seconds from now, is completely unknown. It is the unknown in life that causes fear—and a lot of it!

With all of these unknowns and the fears that they bring, there are some particular categories of unknowns that bring us the most amount of fear. Let's take a closer look at some of them.

> Sickness, danger, disaster. These are things that are out of our control. I can take safety and health precautions, but I can't completely prevent sickness, nor can I always prevent what sickness will do to me. If I'm in danger, I don't know what that bear or snake or bad guy around the corner will do to me. If the country is at war, I don't know what the results will bring. If there is a natural disaster, I don't know how much damage there will be or if my things will be damaged or how many people will be hurt or die. Those unknowns bring a lot of fear.

The future. This is a big one, especially for teens. I feel like it is almost an everyday occurrence that I hear from teens how much the future terrifies them. Usually, the older you are, like juniors and seniors, the worse it is. There are fears about test scores and fears about choosing a college, the military, or a trade program. There are fears about making the wrong choices. There are fears about "adulting" and venturing out on your own. There are fears about taking ownership of your faith in a sin-filled world. Those unknowns bring tons of fears.

Persecution. Speaking of taking ownership of your faith as you go out into the world, that is something that terrifies many people, too. There are Christians in significant danger all over the world. In some countries Christians are regularly arrested or killed. In America though, it's the everyday micro-aggressions that seem relentless—being made fun, being treated like you're stupid, being called out as dumb or uninformed or not "woke." The unknowns of persecution waiting for you can bring a lot of fear.

Death. It's worth repeating one more time. The fear of death is a very real and persistent pressure on many. I've noticed in life that the more real the threat of death is, the greater the fear is. So when you're young, you probably don't worry about dying very often. However, if you're young and you have a serious sickness, then you start thinking about death. As you get older you think more and more about it as you see your years running short. If you're in the hospital or about to go under for surgery, you think about death because you're worried about something going wrong. I'm writing this in a particular time when COVID-19 and race riots are causing many to be afraid of death. But let's remember that the biggest fears with death are the unknowns. What will it be like? How will it happen? What will happen to me next? Where will I be? Those unknowns bring endless fears.

There is one more category that causes intense and paralyzing fear because of the many unknowns. It's not really a category though as much as it is a person, or a being. God. That's right. God. I will even suggest to you that there is no fear that any person can have that is greater than their fear of God, whether they know it or not.

Interestingly, whenever we see someone in the Bible who encounters God with his great glory and power, that person is terrified. Now Jesus is true God, but while here on earth his glory was usually hidden as he set aside his glory to live and die for us. So we won't apply this point to his time of humility. Yet occasionally Jesus showed his full divinity as true God and the people were instantly afraid. In fact, I can't think of any instance in the entire Bible where a human encountered God with his glory and power and *wasn't* afraid. Let's look at a few examples.

Adam and Eve. As soon as they sinned, they became afraid and hid from God.[183]

Moses. When God appeared to Moses in a burning bush, he hid his face because he was afraid to look at God.[184]

Gideon. When God appeared to Gideon, he told God that he was afraid and thought he would die.[185]

Isaiah. When Isaiah had a vision of God enthroned in his temple, he was afraid that he was "ruined" and done for.[186]

---

[183] Genesis 3:10
[184] Exodus 3:6
[185] Judges 6:22–23
[186] Isaiah 6:5

Zechariah and Mary. When an angel announced to Zechariah that he would have a son (John the Baptist), and when Mary was told that she would give birth to the Savior, they were frightened even by the angel's presence.[187]

The shepherds. When the glory of the Lord (usually a phrase for God's glorious presence) appeared to the shepherds along with a host of angels, they were terrified.[188]

Peter. When Peter was called to be a disciple, Jesus performed a miracle that seemed impossible, filling their nets with fish. Peter fell to his knees in fear.[189]

Peter, James, and John. When these three disciples saw Jesus shining in glory on the Mount of Transfiguration, they fell to the ground in fear.[190]

John. When John saw a vision of Jesus in his glory, he records in Revelation that he fell down to the ground as though dead.[191]

Get the picture yet? These are just *some* of the examples in the Bible. There are many more. So here comes the big question—Why? Why is everyone afraid when they encounter God, or even just a glimpse of his glory or one of his angels?

Isaiah and Peter probably have the clearest answers for us. When Isaiah had his vision of God, here's what he said:

---

[187] Luke 1:12, 29
[188] Luke 2:9
[189] Luke 5:8
[190] Matthew 17:6
[191] Revelation 1:17

"Woe to me!" I cried. "I am ruined! For I am a man of unclean lips, and I live among a people of unclean lips, and my eyes have seen the King, the LORD Almighty."[192]

When Peter realized that Jesus wasn't just an everyday dude who had good luck fishing, here's what he said:

When Peter saw this, he fell at Jesus' knees and said, "Go away from me, Lord; I am a sinful man!"[193]

Both Isaiah and Peter understood two things very clearly: 1) They were sinful people, and 2) They had absolutely no business being in the presence of a holy God.

Those two points are the root cause of the fear of God in every instance in the Bible. In each example I just cited, and in all the ones I didn't, the people had a very intense and real understanding that God is powerful and mighty and glorious and holy. With that also came a very real understanding that they were anything but that.

Remember how I said the big fear we all have is the fear of the unknown? Well think of how that pertains to a face-to-face (or even face to partial glory) encounter with God. The big unknown is this—What will happen to me next? Will God hold everything I have done wrong against me? Will he snap his divine fingers and plague me with punishment for the rest of my life? Will God crush me like the tiny sinful ant that I am? Will I die on the spot, and if I do, where will I be after that? Will he merely speak a word and incinerate me in the fires of hell in a flash?

Bring this back to the present day then. Being afraid of God drives a lot of the behaviors of humans still today. Some feel so guilty about their sins that they are afraid to go to church.

---

192 Isaiah 6:5
193 Luke 5:8

Others are so bothered by their conscience that they push down their fears of God and ignore them or sin even more to make themselves feel better. Some are so afraid of the unknowns regarding God that it's easier for them (at least in their minds) simply to reject that God exists. Still others are so afraid of God that they feel they have to do good things constantly to please him and get on his good side. And yes, we ought mention death one more time, that many are terrified of their standing before God and what will happen to them when they die.

Let me take this one step further. I will even suggest to you that the fear of the unknown in a relationship with God is what is driving all those other fears I mentioned—the fear of sickness, danger, or disaster, the fear of the future, and the fear of persecution. Think about it. If you don't know your standing with God, then you certainly don't know how all those difficult life situations will turn out for you. Similarly, the feelings we have been discussing in this book also come from fear—feeling unloved, guilty, worthless, weak, alone, anxious—those also can be traced back to the underlying fear of not knowing how God feels about you.

Have you had these experiences before? Have you faced these fears? Are you afraid of what the future will bring for you in your relationships, your college or career choices, your success or failure in life? Are you afraid of problems in our country or in the world? Are you afraid of the persecution you might face because of your faith? If you have had any of these feelings, do the fear of these unknowns lead you to feel unloved, guilty, worthless, weak, alone, anxious, and a whole bunch more? And beyond all this, have you ever had a fear of where you stand with God now and into eternity? When we have those fears we might want to break down and cry out—*I feel so afraid!*

When I feel like this, I need something different. I need some facts . . .

Fact: I Am at Peace

They must have felt hopeless and helpless, trapped with nowhere to go. Their world was just flipped upside down. As much as they were supposed to have been prepared for this, they were in no way ready for it. And sad to say, they pretty much bombed the test.

Over the span of a few hours they had failed their friend and teacher when he needed them the most. They had fallen asleep on the job, abandoned him, denied him, and then hid instead of helping him. Now he was dead. On top of this, everyone seemed to hate them and everything they had hoped for was now dashed to pieces. Where could they go now? What were they going to do now?

So many more questions filled their heads: What if Jesus wasn't who he claimed to be? What if they had wasted the last three years of their lives? What if God's Messiah would never come? What if the Jews go after them next? What if the Romans crucify them too? Would they have to hide forever? Would their families be safe? Would anything ever be normal again? In the midst of all those fears, that's when the unthinkable happened. John, who was there, recorded it for us:

> On the evening of that first day of the week, when the disciples were together, with the doors locked for fear of the Jewish leaders, Jesus came and stood among them and said, "Peace be with you!" After he said this, he showed them his hands and side. The disciples were overjoyed when they saw the Lord.[194]

After all that happened, after all that they had done and how foolish they had been and how they were now cowering in fear, what's the first thing that Jesus would say to them? "How dare you! I thought you were my friends! Didn't you listen to

---

[194] John 20:19–20

anything I said? You foolish sinners! You don't deserve me!" Nope. Not even close.

Peace.

That's the word Jesus spoke. Peace.

And what a special word it was! You can find the word peace all over the Bible, in the Old Testament and the New Testament. God talked about peace often, and his people talked about it often, too. It was a common concept and a common word for the people. It became so common to the people that they even used the word to greet each other, saying, "Peace be with you."[195]

But what does that word *peace* actually mean? Peace has several different meanings to it. Essentially it is the absence of problems. In a worldly sense, peace would mean no strife, no fighting, no discord, and instead prosperity, success, and blessing. Similarly, when it comes to relationships, if there is peace there would be no contention or beef between people. The relationship is all good, so to speak.

Peace takes on a much deeper meaning then when we apply it spiritually. When we have peace with God that means we have a restored and repaired relationship with God. We are in harmony with God. Even more, we are in a state of experiencing God's favor, grace, and blessing. All of that and even more is rolled up into that one word—peace.

That's the word that Jesus spoke to his disciples. Peace. What is even more special is how he said it to them. "Peace be with

---

[195] In fact even today *Shalom aleichem* (Shah-lome ah-lay-kem) is still used as a common Hebrew greeting. It means the same thing Jesus said, "Peace be with you." Interestingly, Arabic speakers use the same greeting with the similar sounding *As-salamu alaykum.* These words in this cousin language to Hebrew also mean "Peace be with you." Yes, I did feel cool when I was in Dubai and I knew what they were saying to me. Pastor training knowledge for the win!

you." If we dissected that phrase, Jesus is speaking it as a wish, as in, "*May* peace be with you," but he is also stating it as a present-time fact, as in, "Peace *is* with you *right now!*" In other words, as Jesus gave them the greeting of peace, he was at the same time telling them that they had peace.

"Ummm. Hello, Jesus?! How can you say "peace" at such a time as this? Don't you know what happened to you? Don't you know what might happen to us?" Typical disciples! Typical sinful humans! They still were afraid. Luke tells us in his account that they even thought he was a ghost at first.[196] It's as if Jesus telling them he would suffer, die, and rise in advance *and then doing it just as he said* wasn't enough for them! They still didn't get it!

But we can understand. Surely our fearful hearts would have led us to do the same! So Jesus showed them the holes in his hands and feet and then spoke those comforting words again to them, "Peace be with you!" Then as Jesus opened their hearts and minds to understand what he had done in fulfilling God's promises and redeeming the world, the disciples were filled with joy.

Indeed! What joy! There is no greater fact in the history of the world, nor will there ever be. Jesus Christ is risen. The empty tomb is the guarantee that everything God has said and everything Jesus has done is real, true, and valid.

Imagine if you walked out of a store with a cart overflowing with the iPhone 24 (or whatever they're up to now), an iPad, an Apple Watch, a Macbook, a big screen TV, and a surround sound stereo system.[197] Then as you are about to exit the door, the friendly employee says, "Hold on a second! You can't just take that stuff no matter how much of a Mac nerd you are! You need to pay for all that!" That's when you beam with a smile from ear to ear and put on display for all to see your receipt.

---

[196] Luke 24:37
[197] Yes, I'm a Mac guy, and yes, this would be a dream come true.

Turns out you have a supremely rich relative who paid for it all for you *and* you have the proof that it's paid in full!

That's the empty tomb. It's your receipt. It's your proof. It's your guarantee. What Jesus did is paid in full and now belongs to you in full. Check out a few verses from the great "Resurrection Chapter" of the Bible, 1 Corinthians 15:

> And if Christ has not been raised, your faith is futile; you are still in your sins.
>
> But Christ has indeed been raised from the dead, the firstfruits of those who have fallen asleep. For since death came through a man, the resurrection of the dead comes also through a man. For as in Adam all die, so in Christ all will be made alive.
>
> "Death has been swallowed up in victory."
>
> > "Where, O death, is your victory?
> > Where, O death, is your sting?"
>
> The sting of death is sin, and the power of sin is the law. But thanks be to God! He gives us the victory through our Lord Jesus Christ.[198]

If Jesus were still dead, then all the fears the disciples had on that first Easter evening would be valid. If Jesus were still dead, we would have so many valid fears, too. We would constantly wonder, "Was Jesus really who he claimed to be? Did he really save us? Did the plan work? What's my standing before God? What will happen to me when I die? Will I ever be able to go to heaven?"

But Paul reminds us that Jesus *has been* raised. Jesus *is* alive. Not only did the disciples see him, but actually more than 500 people

---

[198] 1 Corinthians 15:17, 20–22, 54–57

saw Jesus alive.[199] This is not a conspiracy theory. This is a supremely, carefully, and well-documented fact of history.

What does that mean for you and for me? Everything! It means that Satan is crushed, just as God had promised in the Garden of Eden.[200] It means that Jesus' perfect life has been accepted as your replacement. It means that Jesus' death has been accepted as the perfect sacrifice and thus your sins have been paid for in full. It also means that "death has been swallowed up in victory," which means that because Jesus lives, you also will live. It means that you have a new life now and an eternal life soon to come. Jesus' resurrection means *everything*. And best of all, it's a fact!

This fact of Jesus' resurrection is what gives you your new life and identity in Christ, and that new identity is what changes life in a world full of fears. Listen to what Paul says in Romans, "Therefore, since we have been justified through faith, we have peace with God through our Lord Jesus Christ."[201] Because of what Jesus has done, you have peace with God.

Do you remember our definitions of peace? Jesus' resurrection guarantees that your relationship with God is restored. There's no strife or fighting or separation. There is only harmony and unity in a relationship filled with blessings of grace from God. This brings us to our first fact:

> **Fact #1** – You *are at peace*. Fears of sin, death, and hell vanish as the resurrection of Jesus Christ guarantees that his victory is valid and, therefore, so is yours.

By now you're nearly an expert. You are a teen Bible maven who is mature enough to know what's coming next. That's right— Satan. You think he is going to leave you alone with knowing you have peace with God through Jesus Christ? You think he's

---

[199] 1 Corinthians 15:6
[200] Genesis 3:15
[201] Romans 5:1

going to just let it be when this is the last chapter of this section of the book and you're finishing with fearless courage? No, you don't think that. You know better because you're getting to be a Bible pro by now.

Sure enough, Satan has his whispers to rattle around in your brain some more. "That's nice that God says he gave you peace. Maybe someday you'll enjoy it. Look at the world around you. Look at all the problems everywhere, including in your life. There's no peace—not for you and not any time soon at least!"

Well here's what you can do. You can just tell Satan to go to hell where he belongs.[202] God has something different to say. In case these whispers of Satan might bother you, how about you listen to the shouts and songs of angels instead. Turn your attention back in time to the countryside of Judea where shepherds keeping their watch at night suddenly were surrounded by the glory of the Lord. They were terrified! But then, "a great company of the heavenly host appeared with the angel, praising God and saying, 'Glory to God in the highest heaven, and on earth peace to those on whom his favor rests.'"[203]

Did you hear that? Was their song loud enough? "Peace! Peace on earth! It's here! Rejoice! Peace is here!" The angels were declaring that with the Savior's birth peace came to earth. Not the end of worldly wars. Not financial peace. Not the end of violence. Peace with God. All the blessings of a restored relationship that we just talked about that are wrapped up in that word peace—they were now here in Christ. That's why he came—to bring peace to us both *now* and *forever*.

It's interesting if you go back and look at all those people who were afraid in the Bible. I mentioned a number of them—Moses, Isaiah, Peter, John, and others. If you reread all those stories you will see that nearly every single time their fears were

---

[202] P.S. This is the one appropriate time for you to use that expression!
[203] Luke 2:13–14

calmed by some kind of gospel comfort. Most of the time you will actually hear the words, "Do not be afraid." It's pretty cool. Next time you have free time (which is after you finish this book!), check out those stories and listen in wonder as God, or the angel Gabriel, or the angel with the shepherds, or so often Jesus himself said, "Do not be afraid."

I think again about the time that Jesus was teaching his disciples not to worry or be anxious all the time. I've talked about this several times in this book. It was that time that Jesus told his followers that they were precious to God and that they should seek first his kingdom and his righteousness. Well here's another little nugget of awesomeness that Jesus tossed in there right after that: "Do not be afraid, little flock, for your Father has been pleased to give you the kingdom."[204]

There is so much wrapped up in that little sentence (Normal for Jesus, I guess!)! First, he knows the fears of his people and tells them not to be afraid. Next, he calls them "little flock" which brings to mind so many comforting pictures of the Lord as our Good Shepherd, like Psalm 23 among others. But then Jesus tells us why we don't need to be afraid. The kingdom is ours. God's kingdom where he rules with grace and blessing—it's ours. Not some time later. Not in the distant future. Now. By grace and through Christ we have peace with God *now* and are in his kingdom *now*.

This is the comfort that we have as God's people. Because we have peace *now*, God is on our side. God is with us. God is watching over us and protecting us. So when you look at amazing Bible passages of comfort from God like the next two, you can know that God is also speaking them to you right now because you also have peace with God through Jesus right now.

---

[204] Luke 12:32

224

Have I not commanded you? Be strong and courageous.
Do not be afraid; do not be discouraged, for the LORD
your God will be with you wherever you go.[205]

So do not fear, for I am with you;
    do not be dismayed, for I am your God.
I will strengthen you and help you;
    I will uphold you with my righteous right hand.[206]

When we know that we have peace with God *right now* and that
God is present with all his power, protection, love, and grace, it
is a total game changer. When we know this, suddenly our
outlook on all the present problems that we have in life goes
from fear to courage and confidence. Take a look at a few
examples of this confident trust recorded for us by some of
God's people of the past:

Do not be afraid. Stand firm and you will see the
deliverance the LORD will bring you today. The
Egyptians you see today you will never see again. The
LORD will fight for you; you need only to be still.[207]

The LORD is my light and my salvation—
    whom shall I fear?
The LORD is the stronghold of my life—
    of whom shall I be afraid?[208]

When I am afraid, I put my trust in you.
    In God, whose word I praise—
in God I trust and am not afraid.
    What can mere mortals do to me?[209]

---

[205] Joshua 1:9
[206] Isaiah 41:10
[207] Exodus 14:13–14
[208] Psalm 27:1
[209] Psalm 56:3–4

> But the LORD is with me like a mighty warrior;
> so my persecutors will stumble and not prevail.[210]

So tell me, my dear teen friend, what is it that you are afraid of right now? Bullies at school? Friends who backstab and trash you online? Failing at school? Not getting into college? Letting down your parents or teachers or coaches? Chaos in the world? Other things?

Take a deep breath. Go ahead. Close your eyes and take a deep breath and count to ten. (Just come back when you are done!)

Let's think about these things. Which of those situations has changed who God is? Which of those problems has more control over the world than God does? Which of those troubles can rip you from the kingdom of God, from the loving embrace of your heavenly Father? Which of those sufferings can change your new identity in Jesus Christ?

You know the answer. ZERO. NADA. ZILCH.

Not one problem or pain, not one former friend or evil enemy, not any disaster or disease or trouble or trial or suffering or sadness—*nothing* can take away your status of being at peace with God. Remember, when you are at peace that means you are living in the state and status of God's gracious blessing because of your good relationship with him. That means that Jesus will always be your Savior from sin, your Shepherd when you're lost, your Ally when you're at war, your Friend when you're alone, your Strength when you're weak, your Defender when you're in trouble, and your Guide as you walk toward the future.

This is life changing, friend. You can be fearless *right now*. You can be courageous *right now*. You can be confident *right now*. You can be filled with joy *right now*. Listen to how the apostle Paul says it:

---

[210] Jeremiah 20:11

Rejoice in the Lord always. I will say it again: Rejoice!
Let your gentleness be evident to all. The Lord is near.
Do not be anxious about anything, but in every situation,
by prayer and petition, with thanksgiving, present your
requests to God. And the peace of God, which
transcends all understanding, will guard your hearts and
your minds in Christ Jesus.[211]

He couldn't have said it any better! The peace of God *transcends all understanding.* The peace that we have with God goes above and beyond and surpasses anything that humans can understand. It's the kind of thing that makes other people—friends, family, coworkers—ask you, "How in the world are you handling all these problems? How can you actually have inner joy even when you are suffering? How can you be strong enough to handle that? How can you be fearless with so much going on?" The world doesn't get it. It transcends their understanding. But you get it now. It's the peace of God which is yours in Jesus right now. That's our second fact:

> **Fact #2** – You are at peace with God *right now.* The renewed and restored relationship that you have with God is yours to enjoy and experience right now and every day. There is no need to be afraid today or tomorrow when you are at peace with God!

Alright, we've covered that Jesus accomplished for you peace in the past. That is finished at the cross and empty tomb. We talked about how that peace is yours to enjoy right now in the present. Any guesses on how Satan will take one last swing at you in this section of the book? You got it! The future.

> What if I lose that peace with God because I do something really bad?

> What if this world gets too out of control?

---

[211] Philippians 4:4–7

What if God changes his mind?

"Do not be afraid, little flock." The kingdom is yours now *and* forever. The peace that Jesus won for you doesn't fade away like the morning mist. It's yours to enjoy for all eternity. That gives us even more comfort because we have a greater perspective of life now and then later in heaven. That's how Christians truly live in peace. They have one eye on peace here and one eye on peace in heaven. And you know what? I have the perfect example of that for you!

I have to admit, I've been waiting and waiting to share the following verses with you for quite a while. I've wanted to share them in almost every chapter, and I've wanted to share them about four other times in this chapter. But now is the time. Now is the time to just sit back, relax, and let your heart melt away as God fills you with comfort, confidence, and courage as you reflect on the peace that is yours now *and* forever. Enjoy:

> God is our refuge and strength,
>> an ever-present help in trouble.
> Therefore we will not fear, though the earth give way
>> and the mountains fall into the heart of the sea,
> though its waters roar and foam
>> and the mountains quake with their surging.
>
> There is a river whose streams make glad
>> the city of God,
>> the holy place where the Most High dwells.
> God is within her, she will not fall;
>> God will help her at break of day.
> Nations are in uproar, kingdoms fall;
>> he lifts his voice, the earth melts.
>
> The LORD Almighty is with us;
>> the God of Jacob is our fortress.
>
> Come and see what the LORD has done,

the desolations he has brought on the earth.
He makes wars cease
  to the ends of the earth.
He breaks the bow and shatters the spear;
  he burns the shields with fire.
He says, "Be still, and know that I am God;
  I will be exalted among the nations,
  I will be exalted in the earth."

The LORD Almighty is with us;
  the God of Jacob is our fortress.[212]

"We will not fear," the psalm says. Even though the earth falls
apart or the mountains shake and quake or the waters roar and
foam—whether those things happen literally or metaphorically
speaking, "We will not fear." Why shouldn't we be afraid? Why
can we be at peace? Look at all the reasons listed:

> God is our refuge and our fortress. Like a fortress, God
> is our place to go that is safe, our protection and our
> defense.

> God is our strength. No one and no thing can compare
> to the strength of the Creator Savior God who is on our
> side. He only needs to lift his voice and the earth melts
> away.

> God is our help. God will use his mighty strength and
> act in his great love to help us.

> God has done wonders. The wars that he makes cease as
> he breaks bows and shatters spears and burns shields can
> be and have been literal worldly wars. But more
> importantly, he has crushed our greatest enemies of
> Satan, death, and hell.

---

[212] Psalm 46

In the middle of all that amazing comfort about the Lord Almighty who is our fortress, the psalm pauses to reflect on peace. It describes a river in the city of God in the place where God himself dwells. God is in that city and it will not fall or fail.

That is one fantastic picture. It brings to mind first of all the original city of God with a river where God was dwelling among people—the Garden of Eden. There was peace in that paradise. Next, it brings to mind the city of Jerusalem. That was God's city in the Old Testament, and his presence was expressed in the temple there. God also brought peace to his people through Jesus at Jerusalem. Then the picture brings to mind that, metaphorically speaking, *we* are the city of God. We are in his kingdom. God dwells within and among us now and we have peace. But finally, this picture points toward a new and better city, the heavenly city, "Jerusalem the Golden." There in heaven we will dwell with God in person and face to face, enjoying his peace forever. Those beautiful verses about the city of God tie together all the peace God offers by grace from paradise in Eden to paradise in heaven.

So with all that knowledge of who God is, what God has done, what he currently does for us, and what he will do for us, the psalm simply leaves us with the most profound words of God himself to ponder: "Be still, and know that I am God."

Such precious words! Be silent! Stop! Cease! Desist! Just be still! Take a deep breath and calm your fears knowing that God is God. He is in control. He has almighty power. He loves you. He cares for you. Be still, and know that you have peace.

Let's go back to the beginning of the chapter. Do you remember what the greatest cause of fear seems to be in our lives? The unknown. It's the unknown about cancer or hurricanes or test scores or friendships or college choices or chaos in the country or anything in the future including our own death—all those "unknowns" can lead us to be afraid.

But now you know what to do! Take a deep breath and be still. You have peace now *and* forever. So . . .

> You have some big tests coming up that really seem to matter. Be still! No test score will change your status with God. He still loves you no matter the result and you'll still be in heaven one day.

> You are having some major problems with people causing trouble and drama in your life. Be still! None of them will rip you away from God's loving care. None of them will take away your beloved status as a child of God who will live with him eternally.

> You see all the problems going on in our country and in our world *and* all the natural disasters that are taking place as these things threaten us with danger and destruction. Be still! God is control of the heavens and the earth. The one who spoke once and calmed the storm can do so again. And even if hurt or harm comes to you, nothing will take away the peace that will be yours in heaven.

> You are concerned about all the choices you have to make about the future including college and career and finally "adulting" on your own. Be still! In every step of the way God will be your refuge, your strength, and your help. Finally, whatever choices you make are all part of God guiding you on the path to life with him eternally.

> You or someone you love is concerned about or even facing death. Be still! Jesus has even conquered death and hell. Those who die in faith do nothing more than close their eyes in sleep and wake up in the peace of life in heaven.

There are so many things that may cause us to fear. But every day we can pause to remember the peace that God gives us now *and* forever. No matter what happens, nothing can change that God is with us and that we will be with him forever. That brings us to the final fact of this chapter:

> **Fact #3** – You are at peace with God now *and forever.* The peace that Jesus won for you and gives to you is yours to enjoy forever. Simply take a deep breath and "be still," because nothing can take that away from you.

Summary

The unknowns of life can make us so afraid! Our minds quickly fill with questions about what will happen to us in danger or disaster, during violence or war, when we make choices for the future, or even when facing death. Those fears can also lead us to all kinds of other feelings—feeling unloved, guilty, worthless, weak, alone, or anxious. Worst of all, we may have fears about the status of our relationship with God through it all. All of this is enough to make us want to shout—*I feel so afraid!* That's when you need to focus on the facts.

Let's review them:

> Fact #1 – You are at peace with God. That is done in the past and accomplished at the cross of Christ.

> Fact #2 – You are at peace with God now. God gives you his peace and all the blessings that come with a relationship with him every day.

> Fact #3 – You are at peace with God now and forever. The peace that Jesus won for you is yours to enjoy for all eternity.

There is no denying that there are problems and pains and persecution, heartaches and heartbreaks, troubles and toils, sadness and sorrows in this life. This isn't paradise anymore. Sinful people in a sinful world with Satan running around will bring many troubles. Yet at the same time, paradise will be yours soon enough. Jesus has won you peace at the cross. Jesus gives you a peace that surpasses understanding. Jesus will give you peace in the joys of heaven.

Do see? This is all yours in Jesus. This is your identity in Christ. Because of the peace he has with his Father and the peace he won at the cross and the peace he freely gives, *you* have peace with the Father now and forever. This is what Jesus does. This is what Jesus gives. This is what Jesus promises. What is there to fear?

Take a look then. Have a sneak peek of what is yours now and what you soon will experience. Catch a little glimpse of what it will be like. Look with me one more time at a wondrous vision of heaven, recorded with words from John in Revelation:

> Then the angel showed me the river of the water of life, as clear as crystal, flowing from the throne of God and of the Lamb down the middle of the great street of the city. On each side of the river stood the tree of life, bearing twelve crops of fruit, yielding its fruit every month. And the leaves of the tree are for the healing of the nations. No longer will there be any curse. The throne of God and of the Lamb will be in the city, and his servants will serve him. They will see his face, and his name will be on their foreheads. There will be no more night. They will not need the light of a lamp or the light of the sun, for the Lord God will give them light. And they will reign for ever and ever.[213]

What beautiful imagery! We shouldn't be surprised that the very end of the Bible and the very end of our story is a perfect parallel to the imagery at the beginning of the Bible and our story in Genesis. The imagery of the river and the tree and the paradise parallels the Garden of Eden, as if God is making it

---

[213] Revelation 22:1–5

absolutely clear to us that the peace he created at the beginning has been restored and will be ours again.

Did you notice then how it says we will see God in full glory, but there's no cowering in fear like any of the encounters here in this world we talked about? There will be no fear of God, no darkness to cloud our view. The peace we have with him means that we will see him face to face and will not be afraid. It's simply ours to enjoy. And there we will reign in joy and peace for ever and ever.

Can you picture it? Can you see yourself there? That peace is yours. The eternal life is yours. The future is yours. It's all yours in Jesus.

Dear teen, trust the facts. Trust God's words.

You *are* at peace!

Part 3:
Your Identity
Now and Forever

Chapter 12

Feelings Based on Facts

Is it wrong to have feelings at all?

Perhaps some might have this question running through their minds. I've just spent seven chapters debunking feelings and telling you to focus on facts instead. I suppose it might be that some would wonder then if it's wrong to have feelings. Should we just trudge through this life like mindless robots with no feelings at all? Is Christianity nothing more than emotionless mathematics, as if we only have the facts and that's it? Should you be as excited about Jesus as you are about a quadratic equation?

Absolutely not!

Feelings can and should be a big part of your life as a human and your spiritual life as a Christian. However, the key for you is to understand where quality and reliable feelings come from. Or better said, you have to put feelings in their proper place.

Earlier in this book I explained why feelings can't be the foundation for your faith. Your human emotions are all over the place based on whatever situation you are going through at the time. You might hear an encouraging message from the Bible, or read a great passage, or perhaps you even read something in this book and those things might make you *feel* like a strong Christian. But at other times you might be struggling through something or hear some really bad news and then you *feel* like a weak Christian. Sometimes you might make some good and godly choices and *feel* like a strong Christian, other times you might sin and *feel* like a weak Christian. Our feelings are like a wild rollercoaster that goes up and down and twists and turns—sometimes in the blink of an eye. That's not reliable for you to build your faith on. That's not reliable for you to build your identity on. Before you know it, you start answering the question, "Who am I?" by identifying yourself with your feelings:

I am unloved (because I feel unloved).

I am guilty (because I feel guilty).

I am worthless (because I feel worthless).

I am weak (because I feel weak).

I am alone (because I feel alone).

I am anxious (because I feel anxious).

I am afraid (because I feel afraid).

That's why we spent time establishing your identity—who you are—based on facts. Those facts are founded in Christ and given to you by Christ.

Now that being said, your feelings are still important! Don't think that Christianity is nothing more than reciting prayers from memory and quoting Bible verses and learning doctrines and teachings, as if your life is doomed to never have feelings or emotions again. Not at all!

Actually, it's quite the opposite. Christianity can be one of the greatest experiences filled with the most wonderful and positive emotions that anyone could ever have. But again, I will say that the key is to put your emotions in their proper place. What do I mean by that? It's this simple truth: focus on facts first, and feelings will follow. I'm going to say that again loud and clear for you to take to heart and etch into your memory:

Focus on facts first, and feelings will follow.

In other words, when the facts of who Jesus is and what Jesus has done and what Jesus has given you have become your foundation, many feelings will follow. I can't say this enough, so I'll say it one more way. When you know who you are—your identity in Christ—good and positive feelings are bound to follow.

I remember some of my absolute worst and lowest moments of high school. There were times when I was starting to feel alone and up against a world of problems—gossip, betrayal, failure, temptation. God be praised that his Spirit led me deeper and deeper into his Word. I honestly don't know why I did it. I can't explain it myself. It seems to be nothing more than God himself who worked in my heart. But that's what happened. I read and read and read my Bible. I think during my sophomore or junior year I actually read through the entire Bible in a year. I was so proud and so happy. I found myself talking about the Bible more. I shared Bible passages with friends frequently. I kept wanting to learn more and more.

Strangely enough (Well, strange to me but not to God!), I also found myself with so many positive feelings. The more I dug into the Word, the more I learned about Jesus, the more I felt strong and at peace and comforted and happy and joyful. If I had built my foundation on the feelings I had from all the problems I experienced, everything would have crumbled like a house of cards in the wind. But because my foundation was built on facts, all of those wonderful feelings followed. I didn't understand all this at the time because I didn't have a super awesome pastor dude write a book for me like this one, but God still worked this miracle of his grace in me by the power of his Spirit and through his Word.[214]

Through the years I've seen this happen over and over again. Focusing on the facts has produced in me the most wonderful feelings. I've had times when guilt weighed so heavily but I read a Bible verse or heard a sermon that reassured me of what Christ accomplished at the cross, and I was filled with so much joy. I've baptized numerous people—babies, children, teens, adults—and struggled to get through the words as tears filled my eyes because I know what God has done in the lives of those people. I've read or quoted Bible verses like Jesus' words, "I am the resurrection and the life," at the bedside of the dying, and I have been filled with thanks for resurrection victory and often walked away so encouraged by the Lord. There are countless other examples.

This is not some accident. I am not just lucky enough to have some good experiences. This is in fact exactly what Jesus has promised to us. Let's go back one more time to that night before Jesus died. As he was teaching his disciples that night, he said this to them:

> As the Father has loved me, so have I loved you. Now remain in my love . . . I have told you this so that my joy may be in you and that your joy may be complete.[215]

Jesus has taught us about how greatly he has loved us. And he didn't just teach, he showed us too. All this he has done so that the joy he has in his close relationship with his heavenly Father can also be our joy in a close relationship with our God. The more we focus on that fact of love, the more joy we will feel.

---

[214] Honestly, it was probably those most difficult days when I dug deepest into God's Word that were the most influential in me becoming a pastor.
[215] John 15:9, 11

Joy is a strange thing, isn't it? It's hard to put into words. Joy is a certain inner gladness and happiness. It's something you can feel in good times—like joy in the blessing of a new baby or joy in the forgiveness of sins. It's also something you can feel in troubled times—like joy in the resurrection when someone dies or joy knowing that God is in control during life struggles. But where does this feeling of joy come from? It comes from the facts of Christ! Listen to Paul:

Rejoice in the Lord always. I will say it again: Rejoice![216]

Did you catch that? Rejoice *in the Lord*. You can find joy in everything that comes with our Lord Jesus Christ—who he is, what he has done, what he has made you to be. When your focus is on those facts, the feelings of joy will follow.

It is interesting to me that very often it seems like joy is the root feeling that will bring so many other wonderful feelings and emotions. For example:

Because I have joy in Jesus . . .

I feel happy.

I feel content.

I feel thankful.

I feel confident.

I feel calm.

I feel relieved.

I feel awed.

---

[216] Philippians 4:4

There are more, but look at how those wonderful feelings that we love in life can be traced back to the joy we have in Jesus. And that joy we have in Jesus is based on the foundational facts of what he has done.

Please note once more (I talked about this in chapter four) that this is not like a light switch though. Don't think that you wave the magic Jesus wand and suddenly all bad thoughts and feelings and emotions magically disappear. Nor should you think that as soon as you press the secret Jesus button only happiness and good times will follow. Remember that this is life "under the cross." This is life in a sin-filled world. That means that sometimes hurt and pain weigh heavily on us and it's a struggle. Sometimes the development of these feelings of joy is slow and steady. So, please, don't worry if you don't suddenly or instantly "feel" filled with joy just because we are talking about Jesus. That's OK!

However, I want to be clear that if you have things in the right order—facts first then feelings—that's when you will start to experience positive and good feelings and emotions. If you have it in the opposite order with feelings first, it will never work. But if you focus on the facts of Jesus first, you will find that true Christian joy will develop in both good times *and* in bad. Let's think about some examples of this:

> You fell into sin again. You've disappointed yourself and others. But you have joy in the fact that you are forgiven and you feel happy, relieved, and thankful.

> You lost your job, you don't have much money saved, and you're not sure how you'll ever pay for college. But you have joy in the fact that Jesus cares for you, is with you, has a plan for you, and will strengthen you. That makes you feel content, confident, and calm.

> Your family is falling apart, and your parents are about to (or did already) get a divorce. But you have joy in the

fact that Jesus' love will never fail you and his strength will always support you. That makes you feel happy and content despite the difficult circumstances.

Your grandma is slowly slipping away, and it seems she soon will die. But you have joy in the fact that she trusts in Jesus, and his resurrection to life guarantees her resurrection to life. That makes you feel happy, relieved, awed, and thankful.

You see it's actually not very complicated. It's a simple formula. Do you want to have positive feelings and emotions in good times and in bad? Do you want to have joy and to feel happy and content and calm? Then run to the cross and the empty tomb. Over and over and over and over again. See the wonders of what he has done. See the love that he has poured out. See how he has given it all to you.

When you know those facts, then you will know your identity in him. That's when you can say things like . . .

> I am loved!
>
> I am innocent!
>
> I am priceless!
>
> I am strong!
>
> I am connected!
>
> I am reassured!
>
> I am at peace!

That's your identity in Christ. That's who you are. And when you know those facts, that will give you joy. And when you have joy, that will make you feel happy, content, thankful, and so much more.

The life of a Christian is not bland or boring, as if empty and devoid of all feelings and emotions. Actually, the complete opposite is true. Your life as a Christian can be filled with excitement and joy and happiness and so much more when you understand one simple truth:

Focus on facts first, and feelings will follow.

Dear teen, focus on what Jesus says and what he has done— over and over and over again—and all the joy in the world will follow!

Chapter 13

A Not So Little Life Secret

I am of the opinion that your teen years are the most influential, important, challenging, and fun years of your life all at the same time. Do you get a sense of that? Your brain shifts during your teen years into super abstract thinking mode. All of a sudden you are questioning everything, you are thinking critically, and you are trying to make sense of life—all while trying to grow up and move into your future as fast as possible. I suppose you can understand why people saying "I'm shook" is a thing. As a teen you are constantly having your eyes opened to the world while at the same time trying to process the world.

However, what you don't always realize is that while all this crazy, weird, scary stuff is going on in your brain, these are also some of your last real carefree years before you are more out on your own in life. That means that while you are *almost* an adult, you can still do lots of fun (yes and sometimes dumb) things. These teen years will shape and influence you. They'll impact your future paths. They'll be full of fun and full of heartbreak all at the same time. Crazy!

I've said it before, and I'll say it again—I loved my teen years and my time in high school. As I reflect and look back at everything that happened, I'm so thankful for all the ups and downs that took place and the learning, memories, tears, and laughter that came along with it all. Now don't get me wrong, I don't want to go back to join you in teen-dom. I am very happy to be someone who just completed four decades on this earth, to be married to an amazing wife with two wonderful children, to own a home, and to have been generally "adulting" for quite a while now. But even though I have a few decades on you, trust me, I remember well what it was like to be a teen.

So I get it. No, I don't understand everything that's going through your mind. And yes, I surely know that teen life is different today than when we rocked it back in the '90s.[217] But I do remember, and I do hear from current teens on a daily basis about what you are going through today.

Knowing how influential, important, challenging, crazy, fun, and sometimes not fun your teen life is then, I would love to share with you some advice. I'd like to start with encouraging words meant for someone just like you—a young person.

Can you try and put yourself in his sandals? Jeremiah was just a youth, likely a teen, when God himself came to him and said, "Jeremiah, you are going to be a prophet to my people. Oh, and by the way, you are going to shake it up for my people and preach my judgment on them because of their sins." Sound scary? It was! At least at first. Take a look at how this conversation went down:

> The word of the LORD came to me, saying,
>
> > "Before I formed you in the womb I knew you,
> > before you were born I set you apart;
> > I appointed you as a prophet to the nations."
>
> "Alas, Sovereign LORD," I said, "I do not know how to speak; I am too young."
>
> But the LORD said to me, "Do not say, 'I am too young.' You must go to everyone I send you to and say whatever I command you. Do not be afraid of them, for I am with you and will rescue you," declares the LORD.

---

[217] That's the 1990s, to be clear!

Then the LORD reached out his hand and touched my mouth and said to me, "I have put my words in your mouth. See, today I appoint you over nations and kingdoms to uproot and tear down, to destroy and overthrow, to build and to plant."

"Today I have made you a fortified city, an iron pillar and a bronze wall to stand against the whole land— against the kings of Judah, its officials, its priests and the people of the land. They will fight against you but will not overcome you, for I am with you and will rescue you," declares the LORD.[218]

Jeremiah felt afraid. What could he do or say as just a teen? Why would anyone listen to him? What difference could he make in the world? How could he possibly handle all this? From a worldly point of view, Jeremiah's feelings were probably justified.

But then God gave Jeremiah some incredible facts of grace to help him overcome his feelings:

1) God knew Jeremiah even before he was born.

2) God formed Jeremiah in the womb.

3) God set apart Jeremiah in love to be his child and to do his work even before he was born.

4) God was giving Jeremiah this task.

5) God was giving Jeremiah his mighty Word to speak.

6) God would be with Jeremiah.

7) God would fight for Jeremiah.

---

[218] Jeremiah 1:4–10, 18–19

The road ahead for Jeremiah would not be easy (trust me, it was *really* tough). But suddenly Jeremiah's perspective on life could change. Now he could say with confidence, "I am chosen. I am loved. I am known by God. I am not alone. I am not weak with God at my side." Those facts of God's grace would strengthen and sustain Jeremiah throughout his life and ministry.

My dear teen, you have many tough years ahead of you. I wish I could tell you that life would be no harder than an episode of *Dora the Explorer*, but I can't. I think you know better, too. In a sinful world filled with sinful people there will be plenty of challenges. You may be living some of them already. That's why I want to share with you a secret. Are you ready for it? Here it is:

YOUR IDENTITY IN CHRIST WILL NEVER CHANGE

Who you are—everything that we have talked about that is all yours now by grace and through Jesus—that identity in Christ will be the same every day of your life. If you sin badly next week, it won't change. If you hit a low point in your 20s, it won't change. If you change colleges five times, it won't change. If you lose your job, it won't change. If you're married and live happily ever after or if your spouse sinfully leaves you for someone else, it won't change. If you die young and in your 50s or make it to your 90s, it won't change. Every single day of your life—today, tomorrow, and every other day—our heavenly Father looks at you with love and is so pleased, just as if he is looking at his own Son Jesus Christ. How can this be? I'll give you at least one solid reason. Actually, I'll give you one solid *fact*: "Jesus Christ is the same yesterday and today and forever."[219]

That verse is yet another Bible verse that blows my mind. One day I like McDonald's, and the next day I like Chick-fil-A. One day I want a wall painted purple, and the next day I want it blue. I change my mind all the time. I can't even write a long email

---

[219] Hebrews 13:8

without likely contradicting myself somehow. This is not the case with Jesus though, nor will it ever be.

Who Jesus is as the perfect Son of God has never and will never change. What Jesus accomplished in his life for you and at the cross for you and in the empty tomb for you has never and will never change. What Jesus did to send his Spirit into your heart to bring you into his family has never and will never change. How God put his name on you at your baptism has never and will never change. How our heavenly Father now looks at you as a little Christ running around in this world has never and will never change. The eternal life with Father, Son, and Spirit in heaven waiting for you has never and will never change.

What an amazingly awesome comfort! Who you are, your identity in Christ, will never change because Jesus Christ never has and never will change. The good news of who you really are in Jesus is not just for your teen years. It's for every single moment of your life!

What does this mean then?

This means that you can walk into any and every life situation with courage and with confidence. You know now that your foundation isn't built on emotions or feelings that come and go and twist and turn like a rollercoaster. Your rock-solid foundation is Jesus Christ. You are built on the foundation of who he is and what he has done and who he has made you to be.

In other words, no matter what changes in life, the facts of Christ will not change. In suffering or sickness, problem or pain, good times or bad times, you can *always* say:

I am loved!

I am innocent!

I am priceless!

I am strong!

I am connected!

I am reassured!

I am at peace!

That's the secret! Who you are is the same yesterday and today and forever because the same is true of Jesus. What you learned in this book is yours to hold on to every day of your life until the day you reach the goal of your faith. And to that, we turn our attention next for one final chapter together . . .

Chapter 14

Set Your Mind on Things Above

What didn't go wrong for Isabella? High school was an adventure, to say the least. Some might call it a horror story. The struggle was real with schoolwork. She actually did try in classes; she just wasn't gifted in ways that other students were with academics. While she saw some of her closest friends excel and exceed expectations as they earned countless college credits in AP classes and put up big ACT numbers, she was just trying to get by with Bs and Cs.

Isabella wasn't super gifted athletically, either—at least not enough to make a difference on any of the teams. The same was true with singing. She always wanted to be in one of the choirs or vocal groups, but the audition part terrified her. If the dog whimpered while she sang in her bedroom, what would the choir director think? For much of high school Isabella sort of felt like she was just "there," present but not really doing anything worth noticing.

At least Isabella had a boyfriend that had noticed her. He was a really nice guy and they became very close. They talked about life and their dreams and goals. Occasionally over two years they even talked about a future together. The thought was creeping into her mind that maybe, just maybe, this could be the one. That is, until he completely broke her heart. Out of absolutely nowhere he did the whole, "It's not you, it's me," thing and ended it on the spot. Later Isabella found out that he had been talking to one of her best friends for a few weeks and even had kissed her at a party. She was devasted and crushed as she soaked her pillow with tears for weeks after that one.

Of course it didn't help that Snapchat blew up over this. Isabella was the talk of the town for at least 10 days as everyone shared their own version of what they thought had happened (although no one actually got the story right). That was the second time she almost chucked her phone out the window. The other time was her freshman year when some mean senior made an even meaner meme out of her. She was so embarrassed!

Yet the most amazing thing happened to Isabella through all the pain of her high school years. One day of her senior year she was looking into the mirror, and she just had to smile. Her eyes were opened to the fact that through this all she had morphed as if a caterpillar into a beautiful butterfly. She had a certain sense of peace and calm, almost feeling joy that she had been through it all.

You see, over all four years Isabella never lost connection with Jesus. Oh sure, she had her angry moments, questioning God and what was going on. She most definitely had lonely moments too. Yet Isabella always turned back into the Scriptures. She particularly loved the Psalms because she could relate to both the pain and trouble yet the hope and the trust expressed in them. Isabella almost never forgot to pray before she fell asleep, and somehow she found herself praying even more often when things were really bad in life.

Isabella always went to church as well. Yes, sometimes she was a blubbering mess trying to get through a particularly powerful song or when the sermon hit home. But she always walked out the door with an intense confidence and strength in Christ, trusting that the one who loved her so much would work all things for her good.

It was the most wonderful moment, looking in the mirror that day. Isabella felt alone, yet knew Christ was with her. She felt guilty over some things she had done and said (especially about her boyfriend!), yet was so comforted in her forgiveness. She felt like she was a nobody at school, yet her heart almost melted when she thought about how meaningful she was to Jesus. She stood there staring at her tear-stained face in the mirror knowing she had been through so much and that so many more struggles were waiting for her in life, yet she had this overwhelming peace filling her heart. If there was any feeling to describe that moment, it was so clear it could have burst out of Isabella's heart and off her lips—JOY.

My dear teen, this is it. This is what it looks like. This is what it looks like when you understand your identity in Christ. Isabella knew the answer to the question, "Who am I?" She knew that no matter what she had done, she was loved, innocent, and priceless in God's sight because of Christ. Isabella also knew that no matter what came her way, she could get through it because she was strong in Christ and connected to Christ. Finally, the most comforting of all was that Isabella knew by faith and beyond a shadow of a doubt that she would be in heaven, and that gave her peace to persevere through every storm.

From the outside, it wouldn't really look like Isabella was different than any other teenager. But on the inside, God had worked a miracle of his grace in her heart. God had given Isabella a faith that was founded on facts, not feelings. You couldn't tell from the outside, but such is life with Jesus in this world.

That brings us back then to one of the foundational passages for this entire book. These are beautiful, impactful verses from the apostle Paul:

> Since, then, you have been raised with Christ, set your hearts on things above, where Christ is, seated at the right hand of God. Set your minds on things above, not on earthly things. For you died, and your life is now hidden with Christ in God. When Christ, who is your

life, appears, then you also will appear with him in glory.[220]

This. This is your life. This is your everything. Memorize these verses. Recite these verses. Live these verses. They tell you the whole story: You, yes you, have been raised with Christ. You were dead in your sin, but Christ lived for you and died for you. Then Christ rose to life so that you would have a new life with him here and a life eternally with him in heaven. You can't always tell. You can't always see it. You can't even *feel* it. But it is a fact. Your life can be identified with Christ because of Christ. Even in a world of suffering and sin, your life is hidden with Christ in God. That is who you are.

And so, as the verses encourage you, since you have a new life and a new identity in Jesus, set your heart and your mind where he is. In other words, focus your heart and your mind on heaven. That's where you belong. That's where your true home is. No matter what you are going through now, no matter what comes your way, no matter what blessing and good or sadness and suffering you experience, Christ, who is your life, will appear soon and you will join him in glory. Oh, what a day!

Maybe you noticed something in the middle part of this book. In each chapter that we explored the facts of who you are vs. the feelings that we battle, we ended with some verses from Revelation. This was no accident.

I shared those verses with you because Revelation presents to you an incredible dual reality. It shows to you the life and glory that are presently yours in Jesus, and at the same time it shows to you the life and the glory that you soon will experience in person in heaven.

Imagine that experience! Imagine that day! Imagine that moment when finally Christ, who is your life and your identity, will meet

---

[220] Colossians 3:1–4

you face to face and say, "Well done, good and faithful servant! Come and share your master's happiness!"[221] The facts of who Jesus is and what he has done for us will fill us with feelings of inexpressible joy for ever and ever.

So listen to Jesus who says to us, "Yes, I am coming soon!"[222]

My dear teen, that is your Savior. That is your God. That is your identity. That is your future.

Know who you are in Jesus. Set your heart and mind on him each day, until the Day he returns in glory. To that we say, "Amen. Come, Lord Jesus!"[223]

Christ be with you, my dear teen, till we meet there at Jesus' feet.

"The grace of the Lord Jesus be with God's people. Amen."[224]

---

[221] Matthew 25:23
[222] Revelation 22:20
[223] Revelation 22:20
[224] Revelation 22:21

Chapter 15

Quick Reference for Helpful Passages

Use the following lists of Bible passages to help in times that you are struggling with certain feelings and need to find extra encouragement in the facts of God's love and promises.

When I feel unloved:
Exodus 34:6–7
Deuteronomy 7:9
Psalm 86:15
Psalm 103:8–18
Psalm 136
Isaiah 43:4–5
Isaiah 54:10
Jeremiah 31:3
Lamentations 3:22–24
Zephaniah 3:17
John 3:16
John 13:34–35
John 15:9–17
Romans 5:6–8
Romans 8:35–39
Galatians 2:20
Ephesians 2:4–5
Ephesians 3:17–19
Ephesians 5:1–2
2 Thessalonians 3:5
1 John 3:1
1 John 3:16
1 John 4:7–21
Revelation 1:5–6

When I feel guilty:
Exodus 34:6–7
Psalm 32:1–5
Psalm 51:1–15
Psalm 103:8–18
Isaiah 1:18
Isaiah 53:4–6
Jeremiah 31:33–34
Micah 7:18–19
Zechariah 3:3–4
John 8:1–11
Romans 1:16–17
Romans 3:21–28
Romans 5:1–2, 6–11
Romans 8:1–2
1 Corinthians 6:11
2 Corinthians 5:17–21
Galatians 2:16
Galatians 3:26–29
Ephesians 2:4–10
Ephesians 5:25–27
Titus 3:4–7
1 Peter 2:23–25
Revelation 2:17
Revelation 7:9–17

When I feel worthless:

Genesis 1:26–27
Job 10:8–12
Psalm 8
Psalm 107:8–9
Psalm 139:13–18
Psalm 147:11
Isaiah 43:1–11
Isaiah 49:14–16
Jeremiah 31:3
Zephaniah 3:17
Matthew 6:25–34
Matthew 10:29–31
Matthew 20:28
Luke 12:6–7
Luke 15:1–7
Luke 15:8–10
Luke 15:11–32
John 1:12–13
John 10:11–18
John 15:12–17
Romans 5:6–8
Romans 8:31–39
1 Corinthians 6:19–20
2 Corinthians 3:18
2 Corinthians 5:17
Galatians 2:20
Galatians 3:13–14
Ephesians 1:7–8
Ephesians 2:8–10
Philippians 3:12–14
Titus 2:13–14
Titus 3:4–7
1 Peter 1:18–19
1 Peter 2:9–10
1 Peter 5:7
1 John 3:1–3
Revelation 5:9–10

When I feel weak:

Exodus 15:2
Deuteronomy 31:6
Joshua 1:9
1 Samuel 17:45–47
Psalm 18:1–2
Psalm 27:1
Psalm 28:6–9
Psalm 31:1–5, 21–24
Psalm 46
Psalm 73:25–26
Psalm 118:14–17
Isaiah 12:2–3
Isaiah 40:28–31
Isaiah 41:10
Isaiah 42:3
Habakkuk 3:19
Matthew 19:26
Matthew 26:41
Mark 4:35–41
Luke 5:1–11
Luke 5:17–26
John 11:25–44
John 16:33
John 19:30
Romans 1:16–17
Romans 8:26–27
1 Corinthians 1:23–31
1 Corinthians 15:55–57
2 Corinthians 12:9–10
Ephesians 3:14–21
Ephesians 6:10–17
Philippians 4:13
Colossians 1:11
2 Timothy 4:17–18
Hebrews 4:14–16
1 Peter 5:10–11
Revelation 7:12, 15–17

When I feel alone:

Exodus 33:14
Numbers 6:24–26
Deuteronomy 31:6–8
Joshua 1:9
1 Samuel 12:22
Psalm 16:9–11
Psalm 23
Psalm 25:16–22
Psalm 27
Psalm 46
Psalm 68:4–6
Psalm 73:23–28
Psalm 121
Psalm 139:7–10
Psalm 147:1–6
Proverbs 18:24
Isaiah 41:10
Isaiah 43:1–5
Isaiah 49:14–16
Isaiah 54:10
Zephaniah 3:17
Matthew 5:3–12
Matthew 11:28–30
Matthew 18:20
Matthew 27:46
Matthew 28:20
John 15:5
John 17:20–26
Romans 8:35–39
Romans 12:4–8
1 Corinthians 12:12–27
Colossians 3:3–4
2 Timothy 4:17–18
Hebrews 13:5
Hebrews 13:8
1 Peter 2:23–25
Revelation 7:9–10, 15–17

When I feel anxious:

Numbers 6:24–26
Psalm 16:9–11
Psalm 23
Psalm 27
Psalm 31:14–16
Psalm 34:17–22
Psalm 37:5
Psalm 46
Psalm 62:1–2
Psalm 73:23–28
Psalm 94:18–19
Psalm 121
Psalm 147:1–6
Proverbs 3:5–6
Proverbs 12:25
Isaiah 26:1–4
Isaiah 35:3–4
Isaiah 40:1–2
Isaiah 41:10
Isaiah 54:10
Jeremiah 17:7–8
Jeremiah 29:11
Zephaniah 3:17
Matthew 5:3–12
Matthew 6:25–34
Matthew 11:28–30
John 14:1–4
John 16:33
Romans 8:28–30
2 Corinthians 1:3–4
Philippians 4:6–7
Colossians 3:3–4
Hebrews 4:14–16
Hebrews 13:5
Hebrews 13:8
1 Peter 5:7
Revelation 21:1–7

When I feel afraid:
Exodus 14:13–14
Numbers 6:24–26
Deuteronomy 31:6–8
Joshua 1:9
Psalm 23
Psalm 27
Psalm 28:6–9
Psalm 34:4–7
Psalm 46
Psalm 56:3–4
Psalm 73:23–28
Psalm 91
Psalm 121
Proverbs 29:25
Isaiah 9:6–7
Isaiah 26:1–4
Isaiah 35:3–4
Isaiah 41:10
Isaiah 43:1–5
Isaiah 54:10
Lamentations 3:55–58
Matthew 5:3–12
Luke 2:13–14
Luke 12:32
John 14:1–4
John 14:27
John 16:33
John 20:19–21
Romans 15:13
Philippians 4:6–7
Colossians 3:15
2 Thessalonians 3:16
2 Timothy 1:7
Hebrews 4:14–16
Hebrews 13:5
Revelation 7:15–17
Revelation 22:1–5